Fireproof Moth

A Missionary in Taiwan's White Terror

Milo L. Thornberry

Fireproof Moth - A Missionary in Taiwan's White Terror

FIRST SUNBURY PRESS EDITION
Printed in the United States of America
February 2011

ISBN 978-1-934597-32-3

Published by:
Sunbury Press
Lemoyne, PA
www.sunburypress.com

Lemoyne, Pennsylvania   USA

For

Peter, Matthew, and Tony

who tired of talking and decided to do something

There is no shortage of American graduate students, missionaries... with both ardent views on Taiwanese independence and a willingness to conduct themselves as if they were fireproof moths.

— Thomas P. Shoesmith, country director of the Office of the Republic of China Affairs, U.S. Department of State, in a communiqué to Deputy Chief of Mission Oscar Armstrong at the American Embassy, Taipei, on March 9, 1971

CONTENTS

Preface

Other foreigners have written about their lives in Taiwan and their discovery of the repression, murders, executions, and slaughter of the Taiwanese by the Nationalist government.

Few of them had known about Taiwan's history before arriving. The Nationalist government under the Kuomintang (KMT) had carried out a massacre of Taiwanese in 1947, which resulted in martial law in Taiwan for the next forty years. United States government policy at the time complemented the imposed silence and censorship of this regime by keeping Americans living in Taiwan under surveillance as well. The recent film *Formosa Betrayed* portrays the viciousness of both the KMT regime and the complexity of America's foreign policy throughout the era of martial law.

The title of Milo's book is a quote taken from the derisive remark of an American State Department official one week after Milo and his family were deported from the island. The full text of the remark is provided on the first page of the memoir:

"There is no shortage of American graduate students, missionaries . . . with both ardent views on Taiwanese Independence and a willingness to conduct themselves as if they were fireproof moths."

For almost twenty years, Milo was denied a passport and not allowed to leave the U.S.

Though now divorced for over thirty years, Judith read and commented on Milo's memoirs as he wrote them. The book reveals how he and Judith successfully and secretly organized the escape of Peng Ming-min from Taiwan. Peng's importance in the Taiwan Independence movement is seen on the island as a struggle similar to that of South African political prisoner Nelson Mandela. The Thornberrys were Peng's closest foreign friends, and they met regularly with him and other dissidents. When they discovered that his life was in danger, they spirited him out of the country, which created an international incident.

Their role in this episode is now fully revealed in this book. It is a stunning and tense narrative of his and Judith's lives, and the risks they took living in Taiwan under martial law.

But Milo's memoir is much more than the story of personal danger involving secretive escape and loss of the freedom to travel out of America to foreign shores. Like a Graham Greene novel, the plot is a vehicle for a philosophical and spiritual journey.

The first third of Milo's book reveals how his pursuit of spirituality led him into a surprising life of missionary work. His appointment to serve in Taiwan was as unexpected as his knowledge of Taiwan was incomplete.

The book could have been called _The Spiritual Education of Milo Thornberry._ Milo's journey through Taiwan's political labyrinth made him aware of the suppression the local Taiwanese population suffered under Chiang Kai-shek's martial law. Internationally, the Cold War focused American support on the anti-communist regime in Taiwan. The Methodist Church supported both the Mainlander Chinese who ruled Taiwan and America's foreign policy goals. Consequently, Milo slowly and painfully began asking questions about the ethical and moral role of a missionary who was dedicated to Jesus' commitment to humanity.

Throughout his multiple lives as a representative of the Methodist church, a teacher in two of the island's seminaries, and a father of two children, Milo was also deeply involved in secret meetings with radical political leaders who represented the then illegal goals of Taiwan independence.

It is important to remember that the sixties and seventies were dominated by the ideas of liberation theology. Those calls to Christian action and sacrifice were suffused with Marxist theories of the human condition that required liberation over spirituality. Milo struggled to find a theological justification for protest based firmly in the tradition of Jesus' opposition to Roman rule.

In the 1960s Taiwan was alight with arguments regarding efficacy and justification for violence. The effects of the massive killings by KMT troops in 1947 as well as the consequent White Terror drove many to consider retaliation. There were still internal political refugees hiding in the mountains. Some of the abused were considering violent uprisings. Others were peacefully advocating human rights. The government severely punished anyone who discussed the events of 1947 or government repression. Foreigners' mail was regularly opened and read by government monitors.

Milo and Judith sought out reliable friends in Taiwan, Hong Kong and the United States to get them through their moral morass—abiding by church and government regulations and yet supporting the suffering Taiwanese community. The book is filled with thoughtful conversations and debates with both Taiwanese and foreigners.

Milo writes in detail of his search for direction and meaning. He orders books from abroad to his home in Taipei always aware of the looming threat of censorship. The theologian Reinhold Niebuhr had been important to Milo in seminary and even more so in Taiwan. Two other authors became especially important for him in Taiwan: Colin Morris, a fellow Methodist missionary in Zambia, and S.G.F. Brandon, an English New Testament background scholar.

The major issue in the works of Morris and Brandon was the justification of violence. And for Milo, the answer lay in asking what Jesus would do. But the message was not simple: "I no longer assumed that Jesus had to be a pacifist. . . . Despite Niebuhr's dictum that the line between violence and nonviolence was not absolute, I personally sensed a chasm between them, one that if I crossed I would no longer be who I thought I was."

As they became more involved with the Taiwan Independence movement, the Thornberrys entered into the dark realm of subversive culture that included money drops, false identities, and devious behavior.

Their greatest coup was the successful escape of Peng Ming-min, and though they were never discovered for this act of political sabotage and heroism, they were eventually accused and expelled for actions they never committed. It took them many years to know the cause of their arrest and expulsion. The answer to this is the surprise the reader will find at the end of the book.

Milo has created a document that should become a classic in both the realm of the missionary experience in repressive environments and the broader community of political activists. The narrative's style is a combination of the detective thriller and the personal memoir. The characters' conversations are unique to their personality and condition. Each chapter leads the reader into deeper domains of the mystery of the plight of the author and the terror among his friends. Throughout the narrative, there is a running theological and moral debate that gives the story universal meaning.

I was fortunate to have Milo and Judith Thornberry as neighbors living just a few doors down on Chi-nan Road, Section 2 of Taipei from 1965 to 1967. We both had an infant child to take care of, and we both became deeply involved in Taiwan politics and the issues of human rights.

It is thus with great respect and even greater memories that I read this story of how he came to dovetail his religious faith with the struggle of human rights in Taiwan.

Richard C. Kagan
Professor Emeritus of East Asian Studies,
Hamline University

Introduction
Santa's Smile

A giant helium-filled Santa Claus bobbed in the wind outside my window at the Ambassador Hotel. I thought about the Macy's Thanksgiving Day Parade but remembered that this was Taipei, not New York City. The crowds on Chungshan North Road three floors below seemed indifferent to the grinning balloon tethered to the hotel. I was sitting on the bed and turned my attention back to reading a document Dick Kagan had given me at lunch—the recently declassified conversation among U.S. President Richard Nixon, Secretary of State Henry Kissinger, and Chinese Premier Chou En-lai.

The purpose of the meeting of three of the most powerful people on earth in Peking that February 23, 1972, was to figure out how relations between their two countries could be normalized. They all agreed that Taiwan was the nub of the problem. In Chou's mind, U.S. intentions for the island were not clear. Nixon protested that he was ready to give up the island as the price for the normalization of relations with the People's Republic, but he needed to prepare Congress and the American people for the time when China could have its way with Taiwan.

Chou pressed Kissinger and Nixon on their promise not to support the Taiwan Independence Movement either in the U.S. or Taiwan. Kissinger cautioned that they could "encourage," but "allow" was beyond their capability.

"Discourage," suggested Chou.

"Discourage," agreed Nixon.

"But you should say that you would not allow a Taiwan Independence Movement on Taiwan while American forces are still on Taiwan," said Chou.

"While they are still there," Nixon qualified.

"Because you know even Chiang Kai-shek said that you let Peng Ming-min out," Chou pushed.

"That is not true," said Kissinger. He then continued to explain that no American personnel or agency would give any encouragement or support in any way to the Taiwan Independence Movement.

"I endorse that commitment at this meeting today," echoed the president.

Still not satisfied, Chou persisted: "I have received material to the effect that Peng Ming-min was able to escape with help from the Americans."

With a show of indignation, Nixon responded, "Mr. Prime Minister, Chiang Kai-shek did not like it. You did not like it, either. Neither did we like it. We had nothing to do with it."

"To the best of my knowledge that professor was probably able to leave because of help from American anti-Chiang Kai-shek left-wing groups," Kissinger added.

Santa seemed to wave to me through the window that gray Saturday, December 6, 2003. I smiled as I thought how Mao, Chiang, Chou, and Nixon had all wanted to know how Peng escaped, but they had gone to their graves not knowing—and not knowing my role in it.

Santa's grin suddenly filled my window. At first I imagined him joining me in my pleasure in having successfully kept the secret and my first return to Taiwan in thirty-two years. While I reflected on what I was reading and the welcome back to Taiwan, Santa's grin seemed to turn to a garish smirk reminding me of the cost, not just of Peng's escape but also of all that had happened in that distant past.

I never imagined that I would return to Taiwan. Over the years I didn't think I would write an account of those events because to do so would have been a threat to the friends I had left behind. After the emergence from martial law in 1987 and the hope of democracy in the 1990s, I was still not sure my friends would be safe. But in 2000 Taiwan had its first freely elected president, the Democratic Progressive Party's Chen Shui-bian, the first non-Kuomintang (KMT) official to hold the office.

At my children's urging, I agreed to write an account of those events, which they were too young to remember. Katy had not even been born yet. The time seemed right. For sixteen weeks, I wrote weekly installments and e-mailed them to Liz, Katy, and Richard every Monday, my day off as pastor at First United Methodist Church in Bend, Oregon.

Although their mother Judith and I had been divorced for over twenty-five years, I encouraged the kids to get her perspective because what we did in Taiwan was done as a team. Judith and I discussed and agreed on every activity and we each fully participated in everything that resulted in our arrest and expulsion. I shared with her the letters I wrote to our children with the assurance that I was making no attempt to speak for both of us. The use of "we" did not intend to speak for Judith, nor the use of "I" to exclude her. Still cautious, I instructed the kids not to share the letters outside the family.

Completion of the sixteen installments seemed to fulfill what I felt was my responsibility to Liz, Richard, and Katy. But on September 25, 2003, I received a phone call from a colleague I had known in Taiwan, Michael Fonte. At the time he was a Maryknoll missionary; now he was in the Washington office of the Democratic Progressive Party. He invited me to return to Taiwan so that I could be recognized for my human rights activities in the late sixties and early seventies. Judith, Liz, Richard, and Katy were also invited, along with other foreigners like ourselves who had incurred the wrath of the KMT.

The visit was a serendipitous confirmation of the story I had written for the kids almost a year earlier. After a few days of listening to panel discussions sponsored by the Taiwan Foundation for Democracy, Richard said, "It wasn't that I didn't believe your story, Dad, but hearing it from others made it more real."

Encouraged by my Taiwanese and American friends who were collaborators in the events, I decided that it was time to tell the story aloud. What you will find in these pages is an account of how and why on March 2, 1971,

Judith and I were the first American missionaries to be arrested since Generalissimo Chiang Kai-shek's forces took control of the island in 1945. The sole charge, "actions unfriendly to the Republic of China," left the way open for the government to release unofficial charges that it could not or would not attempt to prove in a court of law. The vagueness of the charge also left hidden those "unfriendly actions" I was guilty of and, if revealed, would have proved embarrassing to Chiang's government. Many questions lay unanswered for almost forty years, and some remain; but I learned the real reasons the arrest orders were issued for the first time in late 2009.

This story is not mine alone. None of our stories are. While writ large in my life, mine is but a few lines in the story of the struggle for human rights during the period of martial law and in the separate but interwoven stories of missionaries and U.S. government personnel. The liability of telling others' stories as part of my own is that they are necessarily refracted through the lens of my experience. I hope that what emerges at the end adds to their experience and clarifies mine.

Chapter One
A Sunday Night in February

*Storytelling reveals meaning without
committing the error of defining it.*

— Hannah Arendt (1906-1975)

One of the problems with writing history or telling a
story is deciding where to begin.   Being the first
missionaries to be arrested and then expelled from Taiwan
by the Republic of China requires some explanation
beyond the immediate circumstances around the events, at
least back to 1955, when I decided that God was calling me
to "full-time Christian service."

Before the Reverend Roy Anderson asked me to come
to his office, I knew nothing about what was required to
become an ordained minister. The pastor, in the last year
of his active ministry and having served for only one year
at Iowa Park, sat across from me behind his desk. His
office was a small room next to the choir loft with a window
overlooking the parking lot in the back of the church. We
were surrounded by shelves crammed and stacked with
books that reeked of age—a smell I would come to
treasure.   To the brash seventeen-year-old sitting in front
of him, he looked old and uncomfortable.

"Mike," he said, his hands fidgeting with papers on his
desk, "God calls different people in a lot of different ways,
but the experience you had last Sunday surprised me."
He was right to wonder. He didn't know me and had seen
no evidence that I was "preacher material," as they used to
say. He knew my mother sang in the choir and sometimes
played the organ. He knew of my sister, Cynthia, who had
been active in youth fellowship, sang in the choir, and was
sometimes a soloist on Sunday mornings when she came
back for visits from the University of Texas. As I sat there
so full of myself, I didn't wonder if he knew anything about
me or if it mattered.

"Yes, Sir," I murmured, thinking that being polite was good when I didn't have anything to say.

"You don't have any question that it was God speaking to you in the service Sunday night?" he asked doubtfully.

"No, Sir," I responded. Of course, I didn't have any doubts; the experience was real. I was sure. I didn't reveal, however, how weeks before the experience I had said to my mother and friends, "The last thing I would ever be is a preacher." The irony was not lost on me as I thought about what had happened Sunday night.

Papa, mother's father Wilhelm Mahler, had been a minister. He had come to the U.S. an immigrant from Germany at the age of twelve because his parents wanted him to escape the kaiser's draft. In his new land, Wilhelm felt his own call to ministry and served in south Texas in the old Evangelical Church, later to become the Evangelical United Brethren Church, and still later to become part of The United Methodist Church. Thin and five feet in stature with a mustache and a full head of hair, he stopped preaching at the start of World War II when there was mounting suspicion of German immigrants. He and Granny also canceled their German newspaper subscription. Had he continued as a minister, it would have been necessary to stop preaching in German. He didn't think his English was good enough, so he became a paperhanger.

Denied the outlet of two Sunday sermons and a meditation on Wednesday nights, Papa directed his preaching to the family at meals. When my mother, sister, and I would visit, they didn't change their usual practice of prayers before eating; more prayers, testimonies, and singing hymns came after the meals. Breakfast took forever! And it wasn't much better at lunch and supper. There were no excuses to leave the table, although some of my earliest memories were of being underneath the table where, presumably, a wiggly kid was allowed to go without punishment.

Granny was as tall as Papa and looked to weigh twice what he did. Her hair was always in a bun on the top of her head. On the rare occasions when I saw her getting ready for bed, she loosened the tight bun and her silver hair fell past her waist.

Although the nominal leader of these mealtime worship services, Papa didn't get to say much because Granny took it upon herself to speak for him. I doubt that Papa and Granny ever heard of Jonathan Edwards, but years later when I read this eighteenth-century New England preacher's famous sermon "Sinner in the Hands of an Angry God", the voice that came off the page was Granny's. She, like Edwards, believed that humans were under a sentence of condemnation, suspended by a slender thread over the fires of hell with Satan ready to pounce and claim us as his own the moment this wrathful God permitted. Maybe it was because they believed only Jesus could keep us from such a fate that Granny and Papa could so lustily sing "O How I Love Jesus" at the end of our breakfast services. Looming over us above the black veneer sideboard on the wall of that small dining room, I remember a plaque that read, "Only one life, t'will soon be past. Only what's done for Christ will last."

Those experiences made my not wanting to be a minister self-evident to me. I saw nothing attractive in singing about loving Jesus to keep him from cutting the thread that would drop me straight to hell. The rigid dogmatism had been passed down to my mother, but I wanted no part of it. "The last thing I will ever be is a minister!" was probably a declaration of independence from my mother's spiritual heritage. When I made such pronouncements, my mother would just smile. I didn't know that even if I could not hear God calling me in my early years, she believed she could. Years later she shared a poem she had written when I was a small child about how I would become a minister. In later years I would hear in clergy circles about pastors who mistook the "call of their mothers" for the "call of God," but by that time the point for me would be moot.

"You know, don't you," Pastor Anderson asked, "that to become a minister you will have to go before the district ministerial committee to apply for a Preacher's License, get a college degree and then spend another three years in a seminary?" No, I didn't know. I didn't have any idea about a ministerial committee or the years required in school. I would go before that or any other committee because I was so sure that God was calling me. Surely it would be as obvious to them as it was to me. As for formal studies, since my mother and father's divorce had effectively removed me from the family ranch near Clarendon, I had given up on being a rancher. My alternate plan had been to become the doctor my dad had wanted to be himself. He settled on pharmacy because he couldn't afford to go to medical school in the Great Depression. Knowing the years of study it took to become a doctor, the years of study required for the ministry seemed reasonable. I didn't know whether I was confident or still numb from Sunday's experience.

I don't think the old man was trying to discourage me. I think he was trying to reassure himself before he risked his own credibility by putting me before the panel of his colleagues for that first step toward ordained ministry. I wasn't about to be discouraged.

On that Sunday evening I wasn't in church by choice; I never was. I was there because Mama made me go.

"I don't want to go to church," was my opening line in what became a litany at home on Sunday mornings, Sunday evenings, and Wednesday nights.

"Of course you want to go!" she would say, which made me want to scream. My protest wasn't so much about having to go to church but her insistence that she knew what I wanted and her assumption that I didn't.

It was always the same week after week. I would go to church under protest. I can't remember if we had the argument that Sunday evening in February 1955, but I assume so. I was in church that night. I was the only young person present in a service of fifty worshipers; my friends who had been to Youth Fellowship before the service exercised their freedom not to attend church twice on Sundays and were gone.

I sat in a blond ash pew near the back of the sanctuary under the balcony, a full ten rows behind the nearest worshiper. I stood with the congregation to sing to save embarrassment. I didn't listen to the scripture reading or to Pastor Anderson's sermon. I doodled on the back of a contribution envelope tucked into the little holder on the back of the pew in front of me with the small pencil provided.

Without apparent reference to anything in the service, I suddenly had a realization. There was no voice; it was a knowing. I realized God wanted me to be a minister. Despite all my former protests, I knew God was calling me. One moment the awareness wasn't there; the next moment it was. The experience was simple but so real that doubting it never occurred to me. It was a calm certainty that my life had purpose. Instead of graduating from high school a year early so I could get away from home, now I was graduating early so I could be a minister. As the waves of realization rolled over me, I was so excited that I could hardly wait for Pastor Anderson to finish his sermon and give the Invitation.

The "Invitation" in a lot of churches was the time following the sermon when lost souls in the congregation who had been convicted were invited to come forward, confess their sins, and make peace with God. Church members who had fallen from grace and wanted to get right with God again were invited to rededicate their lives to Christ. A third category of invitees were any who were being called to "full-time Christian service." In some churches, the invitation might take twenty minutes with the preacher ordering that every head be bowed and every eye be closed so that no one could see you when you raised your hand as a signal that you were in need of salvation. If responses were slow, the preacher would often intone, "We'll sing just one more verse" of "Just As I Am" or "Softly and Tenderly, Jesus is Calling" so that no wavering soul should go out of the church without "being saved."

The invitation was extended that night, but nobody expected anyone to come forward. In this church few did. But before the first verse was over, I was down at the chancel rail standing in front of Pastor Anderson anxious to declare my new revelation. When he saw me running down the isle he might have imagined I was there to confess my sin or rededicate my life to Christ, but I don't think he had a thought that I was there to announce a call to the ministry.

He leaned over the communion rail and his hand tightened on mine as I whispered, "God is calling me to be a minister." I thought I saw him recoil at what I said. He asked me to repeat it. I did, this time loud enough so that Bertha B. MacDonald, my history teacher and debate coach, could hear from her usual seat two rows from the front.

Pastor Anderson turned to the congregation and said, "Mike has told me that God is calling him to full-time Christian service as a minister." And he quickly added, "I can assure you that this is as much a surprise to me as to you." While it was a surprise to him and me, too, it wasn't to two people in the congregation. Mrs. MacDonald was grinning ear to ear. She knew, even before I started down the aisle, she told me after the service. The other person not surprised was my mother. She had gotten to the service late and was waiting in the anteroom behind the choir loft when Pastor Anderson made the announcement. From the anteroom she slipped into where the choir sat and took her usual place.

After the benediction, everyone came down to the front to shake hands with me, the look of disbelief still on some of their faces. For the faithful who believed in miracles, the fact that it was me and not one of the other more promising young people seemed to add to the magnitude of the night. On the way home, mother didn't say much. Like Mrs. MacDonald, she had known it was coming.

After my conference with Pastor Anderson, he arranged for me to meet with the ministerial committee in Wichita Falls at their semiannual meeting in September. A timely— Mrs. MacDonald called it providential—visit to our high school by Lamar Smith in March to recruit students for Texas Wesleyan College in Fort Worth gave me a place to go to college and a summer job at the YMCA Camp Carter.

On September 8, a week before I left for college, I appeared before the ministry committee. In the five months since the experience, I had thought a lot about what I would actually do as a minister. Being like Pastor Anderson or Papa didn't fit. I told the eight- or nine-man committee that, while I believed I had been called to the ordained ministry, I didn't think God was calling me to be pastor of a congregation.

"What else would you do as a minister if you weren't a pastor?" one skeptic asked.

"I don't know, Sir, but I believe God will let me know in good time."

"Son, do you believe the Bible?" another asked.

"Oh yes Sir. Every word of it!" I said.

What they didn't ask was how I would live my faith. Racial tensions in the South were about to explode. Ten days before our meeting, fourteen-year-old Emmett Till from Chicago, who was visiting his relatives in Mississippi, was murdered because it was said he whistled at a white woman. We didn't talk about such things in church or in ministerial committees.

They talked about my call. While they had heard many stories of calls by those who came before their committee, they were uneasy with my uncertainty about what I would do if ordained. I learned later that I was almost not granted a license because of it. But they respected the story of my call and my commendation from the folks at First Methodist Church in Iowa Park, who by this time had decided I was fine "preacher material." Before the afternoon meeting was over, they relented and gave me a license. The "license to preach" was permission to preach where invited in Methodist churches. College and the seminary would lead to ordination and Taiwan.

Seventeen years later, when I was in the stacks at the Missionary Research Library at the Union Theological Seminary in New York City working on my dissertation, I encountered Eleanor Munro. Eleanor and her husband, E. J. Kahn, a long time writer at *The New Yorker*, found me on their visit to Taiwan in 1970 because a reporter of the *New York Times* had told them that I could put them in touch with dissident Taiwanese. She had just published a book on art in the T'ang Dynasty[1] and E. J. had finished his book on Foreign Service Officers in China.[2]

No one else was on this floor of the stacks, so we sat in a carrel beside a tall narrow window that allowed in a little light and talked. She wanted to catch up on the things that had happened since she and E. J. were in Taiwan. Then she asked if I would talk to her about my decision to become a missionary.

"I was raised in New York City and Cleveland," she said. "My family hid our Jewish heritage from the neighbors and didn't profess any religion. I've always been curious to know what makes religious people tick. Would you mind telling me about why you decided to become a Christian?"

"I grew up in the church, and when I was seven I told my mother I wanted to join the church."

"Just like that? But why did you decide to become a minister?"

I told her the story of my call that Sunday night. Later, she asked about the circumstances that led me to become a missionary in Taiwan, but she kept coming back to the Sunday night experience. She wasn't antagonistic; I felt like she was sympathetic and trying to grasp what didn't make sense to her. A few years later Eleanor wrote a book about religious pilgrimages in different religions, but only after going on all of the pilgrimages herself.[3] I think at the time of our conversation she may have seen in me someone on a pilgrimage.

"Did you believe it was God talking to you?"

"That night I was sure of it," I said, "but who is to say what is of God and what is not? It might have been a decision made deep in my psyche out of particular needs. The only thing I can say is, unlike anything else in my life, a certainty descended that Sunday night that has never left me."

---

[1] Eleanor Munro, *Through the Vermilion Gates* (1971).
[2] Ely Jacques Kahn Jr., *The China Hands: America's Foreign Service Officers and What Befell Them* (1971).
[3] Eleanor Munro, *On Glory Roads: A Pilgrim's Book About Pilgrimage* (1987).

Chapter Two
The Golden Shore

*Does our sense of things reflect their
nature or only the nature of our need?*

— Eleanor Munro, *On Glory Roads*

"What are you reading, honey?" Isabel asked, breaking the oppressive silence of the sterile white hospital room. The intravenous catheter was still dumping chemo into her vein in an effort to stem a bore tide of cancer spreading throughout her body.

"I didn't know you were awake," I said. I could still see in her face the look alike for Dorothy Lamour I had always seen, but now her bare head was covered with a wrap.

"You were really intent on what you are reading. Is it for school?"

Isabel was the other woman in my dad's life, at least in the last year of his marriage to my mother, but I never held it against either my dad or Isabel. I often wanted to get away from my mother, too.

To the Golden Shore, I said, holding up Courtney Anderson's thick biography of the missionary, Adoniram Judson[4]. It was one of the first books I had received when I joined a religious book club earlier in the year. "It's about the first American missionary to another country. In the nineteenth century, he and his wife went to Burma. They didn't expect to ever come back home. It took six years to win their first soul for Christ."

"Uh huh," she said. I knew I was losing her to sleep, but before drifting off, I heard her ask, "You're not going to some other country, are you?"

She was asleep before I could answer. And I'm glad she was. I didn't have to confess that something in this book

[4] Courtney Anderson, *To the Golden Shore: the Life of
Adoniram Judson* (Boston: Little, Brown, and Company,
1956).

had already taken hold of me and that now knew I what I was called to be.

While the path I chose to full ordination took seven years, being appointed pastor of a church as an "approved supply" took only a year. "Preacher boys," as we were called, taking appointments at the end of our first year in college, was the way it was done in the 1950s. Since I had the call and also needed a way to support myself, at the tender age of eighteen I was appointed to Annetta and Temple Hall, two tiny rural churches in the Central Texas Conference fifty miles west of Fort Worth. I lived in the dorm at TWC and went to the churches on weekends.

Only in looking back years later did I shudder at my presumption. The naïveté was not mine alone; it was shared collectively in the religious culture around me. What my ego kept me from recognizing at the time was how these small congregations pastored by a succession of "preacher boys" had their own philosophy. One of their missions as marginally existing congregations was to "raise pastors." It was a charitable way to tolerate the lack of pastoring they got from us.

One of their "parenting roles" was to see that preacher boys got married. My first date with Judith Wayne Thomas was to ask her to play for church service at Annetta, where I knew we weren't going to have a pianist. It took Judith and me a while longer, but the first night she played, the people at the church decided that we should marry. Why not? They would get a regular piano player. However, when we decided to get married, J. W. Sprinkle, the district superintendent, appointed us to Covington and Oseola, a charge that had a parsonage. After such an effort to recruit, the people at Annetta lost both a pastor and a pianist.

Some congregations were more fortunate than those having eighteen-year-old pastors. Their "preacher boys" were veterans going to college on the G. I. Bill. Most had fought in Korea and later experienced their calls to ministry. They were as green as I was about how to serve in a church, but they had maturity. These were men, not boys, whose life experiences with birth, death and dying, marriage, divorce, and the ways society's institutions worked, far exceeded mine.

Since most had families, they served churches with parsonages. These pastors commuted daily into Fort Worth for class from churches outside Mineral Wells, Brownwood, Waco, and Bryan, some driving over two hundred miles a day roundtrip. Some lived during the week in the old G.I. barracks on the edge of the campus called "marriage dorms." They all gathered at the Student Union coffee shop every morning to smoke and visit. I often joined them.

From the start I noticed these guys were eager to learn, unlike me and others my age, who endured college for the sake of ordination. They didn't want to miss any opportunity. Around their smoke-filled booths, they would be talking about ideas—biology, physics, history, psychology, and religion. They appreciated the professors and how they were trying to help us learn. By the time I was a junior, their attitudes had rubbed off on me. My grades went up and I began to enjoy studying; I also began to think that I might like to teach.

One of the things that the people at Annetta and Temple Hall hadn't known was that I was determined to be a missionary—and so was Judith. Before she met me, she had decided that being a missionary was at the top of her list.

When she and I learned that there was a missionary recruitment conference at Glen Lake, a Methodist camp in central Texas, we jumped at the chance to attend. Two of the most dynamic executives from the board of missions, Tracey Jones and Eugene Stockwell, were the main speakers. Their descriptions of the challenges, the hardships, the risks, and the rewards of being a missionary made what I was experiencing as a pastor in this country pale by comparison. They offered a perspective on missions completely new to me.

In one of his sermons, Tracey Jones—a son of missionary to China during World War II and later the general secretary of the United Methodist General Board of Global Ministries—drew on the images of the "four horsemen"[5] to describe not the end of time but the realities of the current world. With stories from every continent, he talked about the scourges of war, famine, and death. He said words about "preaching the good news" and planting churches but spoke more about the role missionaries were taking in peacemaking, agricultural, and medical missions.

Eugene Stockwell—born and raised in Buenos Aires, Argentina, where his father founded the Union Theological Seminary—said that missionaries were needed in other countries not so much as pastors but as teachers to help train native pastors in universities and seminaries.

At the close of the conference, when we sang "For All the Saints", I thought of Adoniram Judson and the call to me through his story. Unlike Judson, whose motivation was solely to win lost souls for Christ, Jones and Stockwell gave me a different view of the role of the missionary, one that made sense to me:

And when the strife is fierce, the warfare long,
steals on the ear the distant triumph song,
and hearts are brave again, and arms are strong.
Alleluia, Alleluia!

As we sang the fifth verse of the hymn, absent was the image of winning lost souls for Christ. In its place, but scarcely less presumptuous, I saw myself in some foreign land engaged in hand-to-hand combat against injustice and ignorance. Judith and I left the conference ecstatic and reconfirmed in our determination to become missionaries. We just didn't know where.

---

[5] Christian Bible, *Revelation*, chapter 6.

Chapter Three
Choices Exclude

Oh, I kept the first for another day!
Yet knowing how way leads on to way,
I doubted if I should ever come back.

— Robert Frost (1915)

At Glen Lake I got the address of the Methodist Board of Missions in New York. I wrote immediately declaring that Judith and I intended to be missionaries. That we might not pass the rigorous screening process we heard about at the conference didn't occur to me. I was called to be a missionary and was a Methodist.

Since I wanted to teach church history or the Bible in college or seminary, I asked why I needed to go to a seminary. Why couldn't I go directly from my bachelor's degree in religion to work on my doctorate? Why did I need to add three years of seminary in the middle?

"In the field of theology," wrote back Paul Yount, a personnel secretary at the board, "you go to a seminary before going on to doctoral studies."

A few lines down in his response, Paul continued: "I've just returned from spending a couple of hours going through graduate school catalogues checking out what you want to do. I didn't realize it, but you can go directly to doctoral studies without getting a B.D. [Bachelor of Divinity). I'm sorry; I didn't know."

Paul was the authority in New York. I was a brash kid in Texas. How could I be right? He had my full attention.

"You can do what you propose doing, and we won't object. But if you say that you may also want to teach in seminary, I think it would serve you well to experience how pastors are trained."

I had to admit that made sense. Besides, five years before going overseas already seemed like an eternity; what was adding three more years?

What I hadn't realized in all the talk about doctoral study was that my grades in the first two years of college wouldn't have commended me to any credible graduate program. In my last two years at TWC, inspired by my friends, my grades improved and I was experiencing the joy of learning apart from academic requirements.

When my mother learned that I was thinking of attending the seminary at Perkins School of Theology at Southern Methodist University in Dallas, she was enraged. She wanted me to go to a conservative or fundamentalist school that she thought matched both of our theologies. My theology, if it can be said that I had one, was in flux when I graduated from TWC. The fundamentalism of my mother and her parents was losing its hold on me, and I didn't know where the new river of learning was taking me. In the summer of 1959 I enrolled at Perkins because it was the Methodist seminary that most ministers in the Central Texas Conference attended. My reason was not an act of rebellion against the wishes of my mother; it was just easier to go there.

I had some anxiety about going to this liberal graduate school and was determined to protect my faith. I was on guard against intellectual sophistication. What I was not prepared to encounter at this school—what my mother called a "den of Satan"—were professors of such deep faith. That first summer I was looking for horns and tails in the form of skepticism and cynicism, but what I found was honesty and commitment. With William J. Power in Old Testament, Joseph Allen in ethics, Albert Outler in church history and Wesley studies, Ritchey Hogg in missions and ecumenics, and my advisor, William Farmer, in Gospel studies, I soon discovered that those for whom the Christian faith was the object of study was also their life. I began to realize that genuine faith did not mean sacrificing intellectual integrity. I learned that the opposite of faith is not doubt, but perhaps certainty.

Dr. Allen's most important instructions to me were not in the classroom. In the fall of 1960, he challenged my class to get involved in the presidential campaign that pitted John F. Kennedy against Richard M. Nixon.

"Decide which you think is the best choice for president and get involved in their campaign; give yourself good reasons for making the decision."

In the first election in which I would be old enough to vote, one of the key issues of the campaign was Kennedy's religion. Several friends and I listened on to his radio address to the Greater Houston Ministerial Association in September, in which his Roman Catholic faith was the sole topic:

> If I should lose on the real issues, I shall return to my seat in the Senate, satisfied that I'd tried my best and was fairly judged.
>
> But if this election is decided on the basis that forty million Americans lost their chance of being president on the day they were baptized, then it is the whole nation that will be the loser, in the eyes of Catholics and non-Catholics around the world, in the eyes of history, and in the eyes of our own people. [6]

By the end of his speech, I was a Kennedy supporter. My contribution, in addition to my vote, was to distribute signs and leaflets.

Dr. Allen also introduced me to Dr. Martin Luther King Jr. Like many others, I learned about King soon after the beginning of the Montgomery Bus Boycott. That was in my first year at Texas Wesleyan College. When I became pastor of Annetta and Temple Hall in June of 1956, the boycott was big news. Many people in my churches, as well as throughout the rest of the South, said that King was a communist. I didn't believe that, but I whispered to him, seven hundred miles away, "Dr. King, I believe in what you are trying to do, but you're going too fast. Slow down. Give us whites a chance to get on board."

Dr. King came to speak at a voter registration rally in Dallas in 1960. Dr. Allen took three of us to hear him. I don't know if we were the only ones he invited or if we were the only ones who accepted. When we arrived at the Dallas Memorial Auditorium, the first thing that struck me was that we were the only whites in an auditorium of two to

---

[6] http://www.americanrhetoric.com/speeches/jfkhoustonministers.html

three thousand people. King was supposed to speak at seven o'clock but didn't begin until ten o'clock. Once he started, he had us all in the palm of his hand. And when he started his "Free at last, free at last..." signature closing line, there was such shouting, clapping, and stamping of feet that the building shook. If that revelation I experienced Sunday night in Iowa Park was God's "still small voice," this was God speaking in thunder, lightning, and an earthquake combined. When it was over, the ethics professor said to me, "I'm glad we're on the same side with King." In the months ahead, King would have reason to doubt that white moderates were on the same side.

As we drove back to the campus, the other two students and Dr. Allen chatted about the evening. I was lost in thought about my great-grandfather, Amos Lancaster Thornberry. My grandfather, father, and I shared his middle name. I was proud of it but had always been glad that the name Amos was not passed on to me.

Amos grew up in a large family in Greenup, Kentucky. When the Civil War broke out, many families split over the war, especially in border states. Amos was the one member of his family that was in sympathy with the Union. He said he was opposed to slavery. In 1861, at the age of sixteen he enlisted in the Union Army, his brothers all joining the Confederate Army. He was wounded in the battle for Atlanta but stayed in the army until the end of the war. He went back to Greenup only long enough to marry his fiancé and then headed to Texas. He never contacted his family again.

I had heard the story since I was a little boy, but on that night, when Dr. King spoke, it came alive with meaning. I realized my great-grandfather had been involved in this struggle!

Marshall Smith was a black Baptist minister who commuted back and forth to his family and church in east Texas so that he could study at Perkins. He spent a couple of nights a week in the quarters where Judith and I were dorm supervisors. At six feet one inch, he wasn't as tall as me, but with his stocky build, he weighed a good deal more. He was one of three African-American students in the seminary. Marshall was my first African-American friend, and I was his first white friend.

"What do you say to Kuby's for lunch?" I said to three of my classmates as we came out of Kirby Hall. A block off the SMU campus, the German deli was a favorite of students and faculty alike.

"You guys go on," Marshall said. "I don't think Kuby's will serve me."

"What do you mean?" another responded. "This is Kuby's we're talkin' about. It's almost a part of the university."

"Come on, Marshall!" I said, but I was embarrassed that I hadn't thought about the possibility of his being refused.

We entered the crowded deli and were immediately the center of attention. We got in line with our trays and moved to where orders were placed.

"You can't eat here," Kuby said across the counter. "I'm German. We're not prejudiced. But my customers...," he said. He paused, and we looked around at angry stares. "You understand, don't you?"

"No, I don't understand," Marshall said.

We left our trays with napkins and silverware on the tray slide and walked out angry and embarrassed. The sit-in movement that had begun in Greensboro, North Carolina, a year earlier had spread to Nashville and other southern cities. In January of 1961, the movement had reached Dallas. Leaders from the Student Nonviolent Coordinating Committee (SNCC) arrived to organize sit-ins at strategic locations around the city. Some students from the seminary joined with the Campus Young Democrats to focus on segregated eating establishments near the university. Every day demonstrators were arrested. Following the lead of Earl Allen, one of the other black students at Perkins who lived in our dorm, Judith and I participated in demonstrations at the University Drug Store and the Toddle House across the street from campus. We missed the day at the drug store when the owner closed the doors and set off DDT bombs on the demonstrators. Students got sick. One of our friends told us that when he couldn't breathe and ran out, the owner, Mr. Bright, shouted after him, "Can't take it, huh?"

As the four of us walked back to the campus, we decided we would organize our own sit-in at Kuby's.

The next day we went back, took up two tables, and sat. The usual chatter in the room faded into silence. The usually smiling Kuby grimaced as he stood by the cash register apparently not able to decide whether or not to call the police. After an hour or so of sitting and receiving hostile stares and words from other customers, Kuby came over to our table.

"Go on through the line," he said.

We ordered sausages and hot potato salad with the deli's signature apple strudel. We got our food and ate. Some of the customers waiting in line left.

Back at the table, Marshall said, "This is good potato salad."

Although this was our one sit-in together, we learned that within a month Dallas joined twenty-five other cities across the South in desegregating restaurants and lunch counters. This was three years before the Civil Rights Act of 1964 made such segregation unlawful.[7]

More important to me than the small victory at Kuby's was the deepening bond between Marshall and me. We talked about what we might do together in the future. He knew I planned to be a missionary and never said a negative word about it. But since I wanted to teach in college, he suggested that I consider his alma mater, a small black college that didn't have enough funds to adequately pay its professors. The prospect excited me, but I was still committed to going overseas. Besides, Leo Hsu had convinced me of where I wanted that to be.

Leo was a Crusade Scholar at Perkins from Hong Kong. The Methodist Board of Missions had a fund to bring promising Christian students from the mission field to study in the United States. He was the only Chinese student in the seminary. Living in the single men's dorm, Leo started a personalized laundry service to supplement

---

[7] *Spartacus Educational*
(http://www.spartacus.schoolnet.co.uk/USAsitin.htm)

his income. Before long he was well-known among both the seminary students and the SMU undergraduates. Leo was more interested in relationships than academics. He exerted only enough effort to make passing grades. It wasn't a matter of intelligence but of different priorities.

Leo taught me how to play bridge. He had master points and was an expert. I, on the other hand, never gave bridge the attention he thought it deserved, and it showed in my game. He also came to cook Chinese food for Judith and me in our apartment and brought with him the only other two Chinese students in the undergraduate school. He insisted that we all eat with chopsticks and showed no mercy. Leo was short and as wide as he was tall, and he ate fast. When he cooked, we soon realized we had to be fast with our chopsticks or he would eat up the food.

Sometimes good friends are quite unalike, and that was the case with Leo and me. Leo knew I felt called to be a missionary, and he made it his personal mission to recruit me for work with Chinese-speaking people. Leo was nothing if not persistent. Finally, Judith and I said yes and I wrote another letter to Paul Yount at the board.

Yount's supervisor, Mel Williams, responded to my letter. He wrote because his missionary experience had been in China. Mel, as he asked us to call him, was already an institution at the board. He knew every one of the board's six hundred Methodist missionaries and the names of most of their children. He wrote that the only Chinese-speaking areas open to missionaries were in Hong Kong, the Philippines, Malaysia, Singapore, and Taiwan. There was no question in Leo's mind about where we should go, and Hong Kong went to the top of our list. Since we were still at least three years from going, Mel advised us it was too early to try to decide which of the four places it would be.

In my third year at Perkins, Dr. Farmer asked me to stay for an additional year and teach first-year Greek. Because I felt the invitation to teach was such an honor, I delayed doctoral work at Boston University. That additional year confirmed my desire to be a teacher.

Boston University had a cooperative program with Harvard and Andover Newton called Missions, Ecumenics, and World Religions, which allowed me to focus most of my study on Christianity in the nineteenth and twentieth centuries outside Europe and the U.S.

Since I had to pass qualifying exams in French and Greek, I needed a tutor. My advisor, Per Hassing, recommended an old man in Back Bay.

"He knows how to get students ready for the exams, and you will enjoy getting to know him," Dr. Hassing said in a heavy Norwegian brogue that not even thirty-five years as a missionary in Southern Rhodesia could erase.

The tutor was in his late seventies. One day, when the heat from the radiator of his small apartment was cooking us, he rolled up his sleeves and I saw a blurred serial number tattooed on his left forearm. When I asked about it, he acknowledged that he had been at Auschwitz and was grateful for his liberation by Soviet forces. Although a talkative man, he didn't speak again of Auschwitz.

"Did you tutor Dr. Martin Luther King Jr.?" I asked one day after hearing it from Dr. Hassing.

"Ah yes," he said as his face brightened with obvious delight. "He was a good student, that Martin."

"I've heard from Dr. DeWolf, his adviser, that Dr. King wasn't a social activist while he was here in school. Is that true?" This wasn't as much a question about Dr. King as it was about me. Newspapers were filled with stories about Dr. King's campaign in Birmingham. As the situation there intensified, King appealed for more marchers to come and fill the ranks vacated of the thousands being arrested. Student organizers in Boston were going to charter a bus to take volunteers. With my field exams coming later in the spring, I declined.

"Ah, Harold is right and would know better than anyone else; Martin avoided those organizations. He was here to study, and that's what he did. Oh, he and Coretta went to an occasional concert, but he didn't let anything distract him from what he was here for, including preparing for his German exam," he chuckled.

"When he was here as a student," he continued, "I knew I would be reading about him, but just not so soon. Within six months of receiving his doctorate, he was leading the Montgomery Bus Boycott.

"You see, these students running around advocating for this and that," he said, waving his arms. "They are good causes, most of them, but they are jeopardizing the good they might be able to do later because they're not paying enough attention to their studies now."

I didn't know what good I might do later. Later I would be overseas and away from the Civil Rights movement going on here at home. My guilt wasn't assuaged when I read Dr. King's letter from jail in Birmingham addressed to clergymen in the city who had issued a statement calling the nonviolent demonstrations "unwise" and "untimely." Like that night at the rally in Dallas, his words seemed aimed directly at me, but now as an indictment:

> I must confess that over the past few years I have been gravely disappointed with the white moderate. I have almost reached the regrettable conclusion that the Negro's great stumbling block in his stride toward freedom is not the White Citizen's Counciler or the Ku Klux Klanner, but the white moderate, who is more devoted to "order" than to justice; who prefers a negative peace which is the absence of tension to a positive peace which is the presence of justice; who constantly says: "I agree with you in the goal you seek, but I cannot agree with your methods of direct action"; who paternalistically believes he can set the timetable for another man's freedom; who lives by a mythical concept of time and who constantly advises the Negro to wait for a "more convenient season."

The certainty of the call to ministry I experienced that February Sunday night over seven years earlier was not in doubt, but where I was to exercise it was. Now, as I approached the end of years of waiting, I wondered if going to Taiwan was a way of avoiding the hard road ahead in my home country and a betrayal of Marshall and Dr. King. I never found any certain answer to those questions. From now on, the answers would never be certainties, only answers that seemed "best" among gray choices.

Chapter Four
Unwelcome Revelations

The mind, once stretched by a new idea,
never regains its original dimensions.

— Oliver Wendell Holmes (1809-1894)

Images of China were at the top of my pictures of the world beyond U.S. borders. Though Americans had had a unique fascination with the Middle Kingdom for over a hundred years, when Japan invaded Manchuria in 1937 we were fed a steady diet of media images (newsreels, newspapers, magazines, and movies) showing the noble Chinese, led by their savior, Chiang Kai-shek, resisting the barbarian invaders. He led them with the support of his wife, Madame Chiang. In 1937 the two of them were *Time*'s first Couple of the Year. By the mid-1940s, those same Chinese were braving not the Japanese but clearly ignoble Chinese Communists, led by one Mao Tse-tung.

For people called Methodist, the message was echoed by our agencies and in our periodicals. As early as 1929, the head of the Methodist Board of Missions hailed the Nationalists with the slogan "Christians Rule China!" For decades to come, that would be the board's portrayal of the Nationalists.[8] My earliest memories of the Methodist mission magazine, *World Outlook*, which had graced the coffee table in our living room since before I could read, was of Madame Chiang and the Generalissimo on the cover. Soong May-ling, daughter of a Methodist minister and Chinese financier Charlie Soong, was herself Methodist. When she married Chiang Kai-shek, he promised her mother that he would convert from

---

[8] Milo L. Thornberry, *American Missionaries and the Chinese Communists: A Study of Views Expressed by Methodist Episcopal Church Missionaries, 1921-1941* (Th.D. dissertation, Boston University, 1974), p. 264.

Buddhism to Christianity, but not until he was properly prepared.

May-ling, so the story goes[9], tutored him in the faith with the notes in her Bible. Three years after their marriage, Chiang found himself and his forces surrounded by a warlord. Desperate, he came upon a small country church and went in to pray for deliverance, promising to acknowledge Jesus as his lord if rescued. Help came in the form of a snowstorm that slowed the enemy's advance long enough for reinforcements to arrive from Nanking. In the face of certain defeat, he was victorious. "I feel the need of a God such as Jesus," he was said to have confessed. On October 23, 1930, he was baptized at the J. Allen Memorial [Methodist] Church in Shanghai.

The story spread like wildfire in China and the U.S. The conversion was compared to that of Constantine in the fourth century and seen by many faithful as a sign that China was being won by Christ. And the first family was Methodist!

When in 1949 Chiang and the Nationalists were inexplicably driven from the Mainland by the Communists, they escaped to Taiwan as a last refuge with a government and army awaiting the right moment to counterattack and retake the Mainland. Although they had no previous work on the island, Methodist missionaries and institutions followed the Nationalists to Taiwan.

If that is not all I thought I knew about China when Leo persuaded me that working with Chinese-speaking people was what I was being called by God to do, it was the core around which all other pieces of information were made to fit—that is, until the day I pulled a musty dark green covered book off the shelf in the Bridwell Library.

In my last year at Perkins, having informed the board that as close to China as we could get was what Judith and I wanted, I decided it was time to read a bit about the land that seemed my destiny, and if not the land itself then

---

[9] The story circulated for decades in many forms. With access to newly opened files, Laura Tyson Li tells the story in her biography, *Madame Chiang Kai-shek: China's Eternal First Lady* (Atlantic Monthly Press, 2006) pp. 95-96.

people in Southeast Asia. There were a lot of books on China, but the one that caught my attention was one with a flyer sticking out the top. When I pulled the loose paper from inside the cover, I found it to be a letter from the publisher explaining how the U.S. State Department had hindered the publication of this book because of its criticism of Chiang Kai-shek and the Nationalist government. Never having seen such a flyer in a book before, I thought it the place to begin my China reading.

Thunder out of China, written by Theodore H. White and Annalee Jacoby, challenged my total view of China. The authors made a convincing case that the Nationalists were losing on the Mainland because of corruption, not because of the strength of the Communists. The book was published in 1946, before the end of the Chinese Civil War in 1949, but White and Jacoby saw the outcome clearly and had said so in the introduction:

> In Asia there are a billion people who are tired of the world as it is; they live such terrible bondage that they have nothing to lose but their chains.... Less than a thousand years ago Europe lived this way; then Europe revolted... The people of Asia are going through the same process.[10]

What happened during the war with Japan was bad enough, but what happened when the Japanese were defeated and left was worse.

It is an axiom that the last attribute to wither in any governing group is its ability to exploit, to oppress, to misgovern.

The KMT returned to the coast from its retreat in west China and proved the axiom, the officials of Chungking returning to "fatten" on the liberated cities and provinces. Not able to put the book down, I read how the people of Shanghai reacted when they learned the nature of the government returning in triumph.

---

[10] Theodore H. White and Annalee Jacoby, *Thunder out of China* (1946) (re-issued by Da Capo Press: New York, 1980) p. xix.

With a feeling of nausea the people of Shanghai watched the government they had welcomed back sell licensees, sell privileges, mismanage foreign relief supplies, and condone hording. They witnessed the printing presses spin off reel after reel of worthless money while prices soared and bureaucrats danced at night clubs and wined at fine hotels. Shanghai's labor organizations watched the Kuomintang hold its first general meeting of labor at a dance club within the first week after victory [and] saw the old opium rackets flourish again under the guidance of some of the Kuomintang's most powerful men. They had watched the government retreat, bleeding but glorious, from Shanghai in 1937, to be replaced by the Japanese and the traitors of the puppet army; now the same government returned to accept some of the most odious of the traitors back into its fold.[11]

I searched out reviews of the book by looking through the thick volumes of periodical indexes and then looking up the articles themselves. I was surprised to find so many respected reviewers giving credit to White and Jacoby for the truth of their observations. Once White and Jacoby detailed how "the king had no clothes," people who had long known this now felt free to acknowledge it publicly. An exception was Henry Luce, founder and publisher of *Time*, for whom the authors had once worked. Born in China to missionary parents, Luce could take much of the credit for the view of China that dominated the U.S. landscape and shaped my own images. But he wasn't the only one. Our State Department held up the Nationalist Government on Taiwan as "Free China." So did the Methodist Church.

"It's all politics," Leo said when I told him about the book he had no intention of reading. "Don't worry! You'll be fine in Hong Kong."

"But what if I'm not sent to Hong Kong? If I get sent to Taiwan, I'll probably get into trouble."

---

[11] *Thunder Out of China,* pp. 311-312.

"Mike, look. I tell you, don't worry! Say to New York that you want to go to Hong Kong. That's where you will be! With me!"

In my next letter to the board of missions, I made clear the order of our preferences: (1) Hong Kong, (2) Singapore, and (3) the Philippines. Taiwan was no longer on the list. I didn't talk about *Thunder out of China* but said that I didn't think Taiwan was a good fit for us.

While finishing my exams in Boston, a year away from being ready for appointment, Mel Williams wrote that the one place projected to be open when we were ready to go was Soochow University, a Methodist university named for one in Jiangsu province in China, Williams' old place of service. I would later learn that members of the Soochow Alumni Association who had fled to Taiwan with the government had established a shadow university to make up for the one lost on the Mainland. Williams didn't once mention my having said that Judith and I had concluded that Taiwan was not a good fit for us. Instead he waxed eloquent about the honor of being appointed chaplain at the university and Judith teaching English there.

"What is this?" I said in disgust, "This is the way decisions are made in the army."

"Not just in the army, it appears" Judith said.

Chapter Five
Another Kind of Preparation

There is nothing so practical as a good theory.

— Kurt Lewin (1890-1947)

Becoming proficient in interpersonal dynamics requires that we do much more than simply read a book or attend a lecture. Increased awareness of self and others can be better accomplished through facilitated group dialogue, the signature element being the "T-group," an small intensive training group in which participants received feedback from both peers and an experienced facilitator. The man some consider to be the father of modern social psychology, Kurt Lewin, established the National Training Laboratory (NTL) around this theory in 1946. Demand for the services of this group based in Bethel, Maine, grew as its effectiveness gained it credibility. Clients included organizations like the American Red Cross, Standard Oil of New Jersey, the Department of Health in Puerto Rico, and the Missionary Orientation Center at Stony Point, New York.

Up the Hudson River, Stony Point seemed a different world from New York City. Unlike the nearby the bedroom communities, Stony Point appeared to be a sleepy little village from the midst of which it was hard to imagine New York City only thirty miles away. Eighteen miles north was Bear Mountain State Park. Stony Point was a town where one might imagine having a retreat center, where one could get away from the busyness of the world and reflect. For almost ten years, a Presbyterian retreat center had been turned into the Missionary Orientation Center, where selected men and women of Presbyterian, Methodist, Reformed, United Church of Christ, and other persuasions were sent to receive a four-and-a-half-month orientation for their lives as missionaries.

Having completed my field exams and general theological exam at Boston in the spring of 1965, Judith and I were deemed almost prepared to be sent to Taiwan. We attended a six-week field studies and language orientation program at Drew University in the summer. I continued my readings about the political realities in Taiwan in the just published *Formosa Betrayed* by George Kerr and a collection of scholarly essays edited by Mark Mancall in *Formosa Today*, both of which confirmed that Chiang Kai-shek and the Nationalists were the same brutal and corrupt government they had been on the Mainland.

Most of our time at Drew was spent on language learning—not Chinese but how one learned a second language. It seemed to me that the program was geared for persons going into places where they would not have formal language training available and would have to depend simply on native speakers. That wasn't the case with Taiwan, where we were going into a highly-regarded saturation program, so I gave less attention to that part of the program and more to reading about the political reality we would face when we arrived.

The most important thing that happened in those weeks was that Judith became pregnant. That our first child would be born outside the U.S. was of some concern because we didn't know what kind of medical facilities there would be, but we were assured that they would be quite adequate. More than anxiety, however, we felt excitement and pride that our child would be born in the land to which we believed God was leading us.

In early August we packed the few belongings we had with us for dorm living and drove fifty miles north to Stony Point. After almost ten years of getting ready, I was anxious to get over the last hurdle. Before I could be approved for work in Taiwan, I would have to win the approval of the staff at the Missionary Orientation Center in Stony Point.

What I had heard from missionary candidates at Drew who had been to the spring session at MOC made me uneasy.

"The whole focus is on interpersonal relations. Don't expect to sleep any during IGR [intergroup relations] week," said one who was about to go to Africa.

"Yeah," chimed in another. "All they want is for you to spill your guts and then they take you apart for doing it. We called it 'Hell Week.'"

"It wasn't so bad," said the first. "They just wasted a lot of time we could have better used studying the Bible and missions, or at least area studies."

Whatever the program was, I was ready to get through it and go on to Taiwan. Once I learned that the reason Paul Yount had ceased to be our contact at the board was because he had been made the first director of the Missionary Orientation Center, my curiosity about the program there was piqued. I don't know what I expected him to look like, but he was sandy-haired with freckles, a mustache, and a goatee, and always wore a wry smile, suggesting to me that he didn't take anything too seriously, especially missionary pretensions. I came to regard him not only as good an educator as I had known, but also with a sense of integrity that made his letter to me years before seem quite natural.

We were among sixty other participants in that fall session preparing for appointments in Africa, Asia, Europe, and Latin America. Living quarters were arranged in six different housing units. Alpha consisted of three separate buildings, each with bedrooms, bathrooms, a kitchenette, and a common living room with a fireplace. Beta was one building with three separate wings and a large living room and fireplace in the center. We lived in an Alpha unit. Our meals were taken in a dining room in the main building, which also included offices, a library, classrooms, and a small auditorium that doubled as a chapel. The participants did the setups and cleanups, but a crew of local Stony Point women did the cooking. We ate well!

The program was intense, including sessions throughout the day and many evenings. Experiential learning built around the NTL model made this definitely not another semester of academic studies. Early in the four-and-a-half-month program, we had IGR Week, led by

NTL trainers from Bethel, Maine. Little time was spent in large group sessions; most was in T-groups. The schedule had us going from early morning to nine o'clock at night. The parents of small children protested to no avail. It helped that the center had an excellent child care program. By the end of the week, we were exhausted from emotional exposure and receiving candid feedback about our how our behaviors were seen by others.

Although the NTL staff was there for only a week, the center staff had been trained to continue the program. T-groups of seven or eight persons—husbands and wives had to be in different groups—stayed together for the entire four and a half months and processed whatever was going on. Nora Boots, a Bolivian native who, with her husband, Wilson, were on the staff as trainers, was the leader in my small group.

There was formal theological study, worship every morning, and cross-cultural adaptation training. Cross-cultural training aims to develop awareness between people where a common cultural framework does not exist in order to promote clear lines of communication and better relationships. The latter had been developed in cooperation with the training given to volunteers in the Peace Corps, which had been established in 1961, only two years before Stony Point. Also built around the NTL learning model, there was already good evidence to suggest that the experiential approach in cross-cultural training, through the use of critical incidents and other tools, worked. This training continued through the whole term.

In addition to the formal program, Stony Point played a part in what would happen later in Taiwan in at least three ways. First, there were the friends made there. We first met some of our best friends and most trusted colleagues in Taiwan at Stony Point. In the fall a number of the participants were going to Taiwan or Hong Kong. Bud and Millie Carroll were Methodists on their way to Hong Kong by way of language study in Taiwan. Judy and Rowland Van Es were Reformed Church missionaries on their way to Tainan. Judy and Sid Hormell were Presbyterians on their way to Tainan. This meant that when we got to

Taiwan, we not only already had colleagues with whom we had shared an experience, considering what it meant to be missionaries, but also colleagues with whom we had freely discussed the politics of Taiwan.

In one case, we learned of a person with whom we would not freely share once we got to Taiwan. Ann McCurdy had been to Taiwan before on a special three-year program. Her friends were among Methodist Mainlanders, and Ann was loyal to her friends. She was our good friend, too, but we never asked her to be a collaborator in any of our endeavors. After we were arrested, however, she would demonstrate what a good friend she really was to us.

Second, I met Joe Mathews. Joe had been a professor at Perkins before I went there, and before that he had been the controversial head of the Faith and Life Community at the University of Texas in Austin. I had heard stories about Joe when I was at Perkins. He was a true "eccentric." Once, when he was asked to introduce a bishop at Minister's Week at SMU, he simply stood in silence at the podium for a couple of minutes and then asked, "When are we ever going to get honest?" Then he sat down. On another occasion, when he was the speaker at an undergraduate assembly of more than a thousand students and was having difficulty stopping the noise so that he could begin, he leaned over onto the podium and whispered into the mike, "Masturbate!" He then began his address to a quiet assembly.

He came to Stony Point for a week of lectures. With a large head of bushy white hair and a habit of wearing sneakers with suits, Joe was the charismatic director of a religious community in Chicago, where members of the community shared their incomes. His theology took society and politics seriously and appealed to us would-be missionaries to take the first year of our service to get to know persons outside the church.

"If you don't do it when you first get there," he said, "you'll be swallowed up by the church folk and you'll never get to develop the relationships with people outside the church who will make possible your doing anything significant while you are there."

What Joe said made sense to me, and I resolved that for the projected eighteen months of language study in Taipei, I would make it my priority to establish relationships with persons outside the church. And I did. Joe's advice at a point where I could hear it was worth the four and a half months at the MOC.

Third, I had a boost in my self-confidence. Even after getting honors on my field exams and theological examination at Boston, I thought that I had just slipped by and that had my professors really known the great gaps in my knowledge that I would never have been allowed to take, let alone pass, the exams. I seemed always to be asking questions about faith and life that put me on the margins of Christianity in graduate school and even more at this program for "missionaries." Not only wasn't I orthodox, but my questions seemed to some as coming from one outside the faith. That proved troubling for some of my fellow participants and even some of the teaching staff. At one point, I wondered if they would decide I really shouldn't be a missionary.

I later learned that there was considerable discussion of that in the staff sessions. However, when it came time for the final evaluation, what was written was that my questions came because I saw issues others didn't see, including the staff, and while that might make some uncomfortable in the long run, it was good. That affirmation did wonders for my ego and self-confidence.

After the pressures of graduate school at BU, the four months at Stony Point provided the kind of "retreat" Judith and I needed. We left the program before Thanksgiving in 1965 instead of when the term ended in mid-December because of Judith's pregnancy. According to mission board policy, we had to get to Taiwan before she hit the six-month mark, making it necessary for us to fly instead of going by freighter with our colleagues. Leaving Stony Point early gave us time to go to Texas to say good-bye to our families and visit our supporting church, First Methodist in Fort Worth. We were scheduled to begin language school in Taipei immediately after the New Year in 1966.

Chapter Six
Arrival at Last

*Culture shock is precipitated by the anxiety that
results from losing all familiar signs and symbols of
social intercourse.*

— Kalervo Oberg (1901-1973)

Soon after arriving in Taiwan, I discovered that the
distance between exhilaration and suffocation is short. At
Stony Point, we had learned about the five stages of culture
shock and did critical incident exercises imagining what we
would experience and how we might react. We were warned
that everyone didn't experience culture shock in the same
way or in the same sequence. But it is one thing to know
all that in your head and another to experience it.

The first stage is euphoria and excitement with
everything new. That's why it's called the "honeymoon
stage." On the first night in Taiwan, I was too numb to feel
anything. After a night in Hong Kong and the day before
that the long flight on a Pan Am 1 from Honolulu, I was
both exhilarated and exhausted.

Leo and his new wife Christina met our plane in Hong
Kong. Leo saying over and over, "Mike, you are here! You
are here! See, I told you!" neglecting to mention that "here"
was supposed to be Hong Kong and not Taiwan. Aside from
his delight in receiving us as old friends, I suspect that he
was also proud that he had recruited a couple of
missionaries for the Chinese people.

When we arrived at Sung Shan Airport Friday evening,
the Methodist missionary community showed up to greet
us. Out of the blur of faces and handshakes the face of one
who seemed to take charge appeared.

"We've got to get you to Number 9 so you can get some
rest," said the shapely, dark-haired Beth Ury. Her
husband, Bill, dressed in a blue suit and a head taller than

the rest of the missionaries, extended his hand and led us through the crowd of well-wishers to their car outside. Bill and Beth were "port hosts" for the Methodist mission. They were the official greeters for Methodist visitors, and in our case they had an additional assignment as the "host family" for us during our first weeks on the island.

They drove us to Number 9 Chi Nan Road, a Japanese house owned by the mission and used primarily by new personnel doing language study. It would be our home for the next eighteen months. Beth rarely stopped talking, but she and Bill told us only what we needed to know for the immediate time. They gave us a tour of house, gave us their phone number, and said that when we were up and about on Saturday they would take us to breakfast.

I saw them out, locked the gate as instructed, and started back inside. I noticed that the house was surrounded by six-foot walls with broken glass imbedded in the top, like the houses across the street and on both sides. The gate was only six or eight feet from the two steps that led up to the front door.

Ceramic tiles covered the roof of the wooden structure sitting on blocks. Inside, the walls were paper and the floors bare wood. It was customary to remove one's shoes at a bench inside the front door and put on slippers.

We laid thick quilts on the bed and tried to sleep. Despite weariness, sleep did not come easily; and then we were roused at midnight by firecrackers. The fact that it was the Western and not the Chinese New Year made little difference. The night of firecrackers was almost as loud and continuous as it would be on the Chinese New Year a month or so away.

The lack of sleep was more than matched by the euphoria we felt in our new surroundings. At about nine o'clock we called Beth, and they came to take us to breakfast. As we drove through the city, they pointed out various landmarks that would help us get around on our own. On Chung Shan North Road, Bill pulled up to the gate of a military installation and showed some kind of pass to a U.S. soldier, who waved us inside.

"We thought we would bring you to the Officer's Club, where you can get an American breakfast and not have to worry about what will happen to your stomach," Beth said, grimacing at the thought of what might happen if we ate Chinese food for breakfast.

Inside, we were served by Chinese waiters, but the food was definitely American. Over the next few days, while Beth was arranging for an amah to live at the house and cook for us, they brought us to the club for most of our meals. Part of our new environment was the U.S. military presence with as many comforts of home as possible in the middle of a non-American city. Since I had no previous experience with the U.S. military, being inside this base was as new as being in Taiwan.

I ate these American meals gratefully, but I couldn't help wondering how the people of Taiwan viewed these enclaves of privilege for Westerners. Most were doubtless grateful for the presence of the U.S. military shielding the island from invasion by the Communists, but what did they think about missionaries having access to these bases? Were we seen as part of the U.S. government presence? Was our access to the base seen as a legacy of the extraterritoriality provisions that provided foreigners with special status forced on China in the hated unequal treaties of the nineteenth century and terminated only at the end of World War II?

Those were my questions, but I did not ask the Urys. I didn't want to criticize their gracious hospitality, and I suspected I might not like the answer I heard. I asked about Japanese houses in a "Chinese" country.

"Oh," Bill said as we drove back to the house, "these houses date back to the fifty years before 1945, when Taiwan was a colony of Japan."

"They were designed to minimize damage in earthquakes," he went on. "Taiwan, like Japan, has earthquakes almost every day, but you rarely feel them. Several times a year quakes do extensive damage."

"How does the design help?" I asked.

"Japanese houses are built with a lot of give. The top framework can move without collapsing, and the whole house can move on its block footings without breaking up."

"But there is a danger," piped up Beth, "and that is getting hit by falling roof tiles if you happen to be outside. When there is an earthquake, it is safer to stay inside a Japanese-style house. Unlike both traditional and Western-style houses made of bricks and mortar, like the one we live in out in Shih Lin, in a serious earthquake you need to get outside."

The first earthquake Judith and I felt happened a couple of weeks later, the night Judy and Sid Hormell arrived in Taiwan. These Presbyterian missionaries with whom we had become friends at Stony Point stayed at our house their first night. We were all in bed when things began to rattle and shake. Sid came running out of his bedroom shouting "Earthquake! We've got to get out of here!" and ran to the front door. Luckily, he couldn't get it unlocked. By the time he did, the quake had stopped, and he was spared of the possibility of injury by tiles sliding off the roof.

Earthquakes I had expected; the cold I hadn't. With no heat in the house in Taiwan and the temperature staying at fifty degrees day and night with humidity at 80 to 90 percent, the cold was bone-chilling, and there was no way to get warm except in bed under a lot of blankets. That was pretty much the weather pattern I experienced in January, February, and March in Taipei. Japanese houses were not designed to keep out cold. Air moved in from outside the house at will.

Light bulbs were set on the closet floors with wire net around them to prevent a fire. Without these lights, within days a layer of gray mold was sure to grow on shoes and most anything else in the closet. Perhaps it was not so different from being in Key West, Florida, in the winter without any heat source. The Tropic of Cancer, which marks the boundary between temperate and tropical climates, cuts across the island, leaving the southern 40 percent of the island in the tropics. The same line runs between Key West and the northern coast of Cuba. I bought a Chinese quilted robe. When I sat at my desk in a room overlooking our front wall and tried to write or hold my Chinese language books open, sometimes my hands got so cold that I had to put them in my sleeves.

In the first two weeks in the country, the Urys gave us a close view of the world of expatriate U.S. citizens living in Taiwan. After the second week, though, they no longer contacted us, but they responded to our calls for help.

One of our calls for help was to interpret for a problem with our amah. Su Su-ching was an older woman from Nanking married to a retired soldier who lived in a wooden dorm with other retired military families a few blocks away. Every day it seemed Su-ching increased the amount of food she served. And being brought up to clean my plate, I ate the increase. Judith called Beth in frustration because she had asked Su-ching why she was serving so much food. We might have been able to ask the question in Chinese, but we were certain we didn't have enough of the language to understand her answer.

Beth came and talked with Su-ching. In a few minutes, Beth diplomatically explained that in Taiwan, if everything is eaten at the end of the meal, it means that there was not enough prepared and the cook loses face. Since I cleaned up the delicious Chinese dishes she prepared every day, Su-ching had no option but to cook more the next day. Once Beth explained it, there were knowing nods, slight bows, and smiles all around. Afterward, I changed my behavior and left some food on the serving dishes at the end of each meal.

Beginning the Monday after we arrived, we walked four blocks to the Taipei Language Institute on Nan Ching East Road. We attended Mandarin classes from half past seven to half past twelve five days a week. In the afternoon and evening, there was homework. The walks back and forth to school provided unfettered access to our new environment.

Coming out of our gate, we turned right to get to the thoroughfare that would lead us to the language school. In front of the wall of the house next door to ours and over the benjo ditch that ran along the wall was a shack no more than four feet wide and six feet long, where a family of four lived. I learned that they had a kind of squatter rights. Similar constructions could be found on most streets.

Everything was so new that my senses were oversaturated, but none more than the olfactory sense. What Beth described as the "rich smells of China" were actually those of open sewers and smoke from the charcoal fires that every family used to cook on, as well as the smells of food cooking. These overpowering smells made us aware of how sterile, comparatively speaking, the environment was that we were used to in the United States. You knew when the "honey buckets" came by. Human feces were collected and used as fertilizer on the farms around the city.

The only thing stronger than the smell of a pig farm came from the ch'ou tofu wagon when it came down the street. "Rotten" or "stinky" bean curd was fried in deep fat in a vat at the top of what looked like a pot-bellied stove on wheels. With a brown crust on the outside, the curd was then wrapped in old newspaper. If you wanted, a thick red fermented hot sauce put was served on the side. The smell was so overpowering that I walked on the other side of the street to get as far away from the wagon as possible. After months of hearing my language teachers extol this delicacy, I finally tried it. The fiery garlic-saturated sauce offset a little of what tasted like Limburger cheese. Unlike anything else I've ever eaten, the taste stayed with me for days.

The newness was exciting, but with it came a feeling I can only describe as suffocation. Except for the English spoken by the missionary community and a few other expatriate friends, we totally immersed in a Chinese language learning situation. We were required to use whatever we had learned in school on the street—making purchases and giving instructions to pedicabs and cab drivers. At home we struggled to make sense of what callers would say after answering the phone correctly with "Wei!" Understanding little and the inability to make myself understood was a frustration that I knew was supposed to drive me to learn faster. But I felt as if I were in a linguistic vacuum.

My pitifully limited Mandarin in an alien culture was not the only reason for feeling isolated; I also felt closed in by the atmosphere of the expatriate community on whom, like a baby to its mother, I was dependent. At missionary meetings, which never included Chinese leaders in the church, I learned that talk of politics was not permitted.

One day, with a casual tone in which she might have been reporting a trip to the market, Beth mentioned that Su-ching had told her that she had been taken down to the police station and questioned for over an hour about Judith and me. At the next missionary I meeting, I reported the incident and asked no one in particular, "Is that standard procedure here?"

Not answering my question, a senior missionary responded, "We don't talk about such things. We are guests in this country, and guests don't offend their hosts by getting involved in politics." As the newest members of the missionary community, I assumed that he wanted to make sure Judith and I got the point. "One person can jeopardize our entire mission."

After a tense silence, Beth said, "Of course they question all of our amahs. It's just the way they do things here. It's nothing to worry about."

There was a certain logic in the idea that it was inappropriate for foreigners to get involved in the politics of their host country. And over the years, I had agreed with it. But with my own government and church already supporting the government in power, I was beginning to see that the question was not nearly as simple as I had once imagined. I didn't say more; it seemed I had already said too much.

I reflected later that the senior missionary was right about indiscrete speech or actions threatening the entire mission. Methodists in Taiwan were almost exclusively made up of Mainlanders who had followed the Nationalist government in 1949, and there had been no serious effort to bring in the Taiwanese, who made up the majority population. It would have been a hard sell because the lay leadership of the Methodist churches and chapels were well-connected in the government, and most were members of the Kuomintang. As a board of missions report in 1967 admitted, since its beginnings in 1953, the Methodist Church in Taiwan had been a "chaplaincy" to expatriate Mainlanders. Given the close ties between the Methodist Church in Taiwan, the Chiang family, and the Nationalist government, the Methodist mission was especially sensitive about indiscrete speech or actions.

There were, of course, other missionaries in the group who felt as suffocated as I did. They had learned to hold their tongues, as I had, at least in mission meetings.

Because of the lack of language skills and a determination not to get involved in the local church while in full-time Mandarin study, I often attended the Taipei International Church that had recently moved from the Wesley Church to the Taipei Masonic Temple. The idea of worshiping in a masonic temple was a bit strange to me, but it was preferable to worshiping at the Wesley Church, the "mother" Methodist Church in Taiwan.

What I found at the International Church was a collection of expatriates, mostly American, who were business people, U.S. government employees, and missionaries who didn't have assignments that put them in Chinese churches on Sunday.

Missionaries lived double lives—their lives working with the Chinese and their lives identifying with other missionaries and Americans. Rarely did these lives overlap socially. I observed that many missionaries spent a minimum of time with the Chinese and a maximum with other Americans. There were others whose whole focus was on the people they came to serve. They won my admiration, and I was determined to be among them.

On my first visit to the International Church, I met Wayne and Jane McKeel, a couple about the same age as Judith and me who had come from Methodist origins in Tennessee. Wayne was a member of the USAID delegation. He was full of questions and not satisfied with half-answers. By the time we had had coffee after church a couple of times, I knew we would be good friends. Wayne talked freely about his frustrations dealing with both the U.S. and GRC bureaucracies. I found it easy to talk with both Wayne and Jane about my feelings of suffocation in the missionary community and not being free to talk about the things that concerned me. Exchanging ideas with people who were knowledgeable about the situation in Taiwan and U.S. State Department policies provided delicious fresh air in which I could intellectually breathe. In time, the McKeels became more than good friends; they became collaborators.

More than these new friends, the supreme moment of exhilaration in those early months was the birth of our first child. On April 9, 1966, after a long labor at the Country Hospital on Hsin Yi Road, I saw first as she emerged tiny fingers and toes. The thrill was beyond description. We had already picked the name, Elizabeth Wayne—Elizabeth for her two grandmothers and Wayne for her mother, maternal grandmother, and great-grandmother. She soon had a Chinese name as well, "T'ang Li-hwa"—T'ang for our family name and Li-hwa, which means "Beautiful Flower." It wasalso the name of a famous Chinese movie star.

We had a family name because Dr. Stone, president of Soochow University, gave it to me. He told me that one of his jobs was to give Methodist missionaries their Chinese names. He thought about mine for a few days and then called me back out to the university.

"Your surname should be T'ang for the dynasty regarded by historians as the high point of Chinese civilization." He had written the character and the Romanization for it on a piece of paper, which he then slid across the desk for me to see.

"Your personal name should be P'ei-li, which means "to nurture culture." I give you that name because that is what you will do here in Taiwan," the old gentleman said, writing the two characters after the first and their Romanization on the card.

The teachers at the language school told me that I had been given an excellent name—one that had a good meaning and that sounded something like the English.

When I told them who had given it to me, they oohed and ahhed, saying that he was known for giving good names. I hoped I could live up to the promise of the name and Dr. Stone's high expectations.

Chapter Seven
Signs and Portents

We are born at a given moment, in a given place and,
like vintage years of wine, we have the qualities of
the year and season of which we are born.
— Carl Jung (1875-1961)

Astrologists look at the position of the planets when children are born to see what forces may shape them. It made more sense to me to look at what was happening when a child was born to see how these events might shape that life. It was not surprising that in those first weeks of Elizabeth's life I thought about the current events that might affect her life.

I confess, however, that the musings were not simply about Elizabeth. Her birth coincided with the beginning of my life in Taiwan. At the time of her beginnings, I saw my beginning a new life in Taiwan. As she snuggled in my arms holding my finger with more than usual interest, I wondered what "signs and portents" in the heavens or headlines were there for her and me.

Since we rarely sense the importance of events as they happen around us—the bombing of Pearl Harbor in December of 1941 and the September 11 attacks being notable exceptions—it is usually in retrospect that we see meaning for us in the events that surrounded our births, or in my case a rebirth in Taiwan. Seeing from the present was a limitation, but no more than the sources of news available to me were. I was unable to read the local newspapers in Chinese; and the local English language paper, *China Post,* was hardly better than nothing. The *China Post* was the propaganda the KMT wanted foreigners to know. A surprisingly better source turned out to be U.S. Armed Forces Radio and the newspaper *Stars and Stripes.* I saw the latter on occasion, but both of them were so much less censored than any other source of news to which I had access that they stood out as beacons of reliability. We subscribed to the Asian edition of *Time*. For the most part, Henry Luce saw to it that there was nothing offensive to the Republic of China within the covers, but when I received my first issue I found where pages had been not so neatly removed by the censors' razor blades.

No media escaped the censors' attention. One of the first movies we went to see was *The Sound of Music* with Julie Andrews. The film we saw lasted only forty-five minutes; we thought it was to be nearly three hours. We came out of the theater thinking the movie didn't make any sense at all and wondered why it was receiving so many rave reviews in the U.S. We learned that the censors had removed all references to, scenes of, and songs about people escaping to the mountains.

Despite the limitations for sources of "signs or portents," I had begun to do what everybody else seemed to do—take kernels of information, compensate for their source, and imagine what might be the truth. With such filters in place, I put together a list of events I imagined might be important to baby Elizabeth and me.

The National Organization for Women was chartered in 1966. President Lyndon Johnson saw to the passage of Medicare, and the Supreme Court issued its Miranda ruling, which would change the way police could arrest suspects. On May 30, the Surveyor was the first spaceship to land safely on the moon, preparing the way for the Apollo landing with humans aboard on June 20, 1969.

In May, a song by Sergeant Barry Sadler was released and by the end of the year, his "Ballad of the Green Berets" would be the most popular song of the year. That song reflected much of the mood of the U.S. Early in the year there were twenty thousand U.S. combat soldiers in Vietnam. By the end of the year there would be over four hundred thousand, President Johnson having decided that he wouldn't be the "first president to lose a war." Antiwar protests were beginning in all major cities.

On May 16, 1966, slightly over a month after the birth of Elizabeth, the chairman of the Communist Party of China, Mao Tse-tung, launched the Cultural Revolution.

Alleging that liberal bourgeoisie elements were dominating the party and insisting that they needed to be removed through a post-revolutionary class struggle, he mobilized China's youth around the country, who formed groups called Red Guards. What was not clear in those early weeks was how the Cultural Revolution would result in population dislocation and anti-intellectual persecution on a scale unimaginable in most of the rest of the world.

While it was a field day for propagandists in the KMT and a distraction from reality in Taiwan, from its earliest days the Cultural Revolution frightened much of the rest of the world. In the United States, that fear would contribute mightily to its blindness toward the possibility of intervention in Vietnam and the reluctance to see Chiang Kai-shek and his Nationalist government in Taiwan as anything other than one more means to resist the Communist advance. That much seemed clear to me even in the early months. What this all meant to the Taiwanese I was not yet in a position to see.

I knew from my readings before arriving in Taiwan the distinction between "Taiwanese" and "Mainlanders." "Taiwanese" referred to the twelve million ethnic Chinese whose ancestors had come to the island in the seventeenth and eighteenth centuries, especially from Fujen province and the rest of southeast China. "Mainlanders" were the one to two million Chinese who had come after World War II, especially those who came with the Nationalists (soldiers, government workers, and people rich enough to flee) after their defeat by the Chinese Communists on the Mainland in 1949. The several hundred thousand "native" Taiwanese, people of Malay-Polynesian descent, were the first known inhabitants of the island.

When I accepted the board's assignment to Taiwan, I was supposed to be appointed chaplain at Soochow University. When I arrived I found that another Methodist missionary, Don MacInnis, had been appointed to the position. The university decided not to wait another eighteen months while I was doing language study. I was relieved. Soochow was a Mainlander institution for Mainlanders. When I learned that there was a need for a church history teacher at Taiwan Theological College and that they had tentatively been promised one by the Methodist Mission Board, I thought that was more to my liking. First, I would be able to teach in a seminary. Second, I would be teaching in a Presbyterian (hence "Taiwanese") institution.

Presbyterians had been in Taiwan almost a hundred years, and Roman Catholics before them. As a result of old comity agreements that assigned different denominations different parts of a "mission" country, British Presbyterians began in the south and Canadian Presbyterians in the north. The Presbyterian Church of Taiwan was the result of their efforts, and it was the Church of the Taiwanese. The first school, the first hospital, and the first printing press on the island were all established by the Presbyterian church.

During the Japanese colonial period, in spite of strong pressure from the authorities to use Japanese, the Presbyterian church continued to use the Taiwanese language in its activities. When all foreign missionaries were expelled by Japan in the late 1930s, the church experienced complete independence of missionary control. Missionaries were welcomed back at the end of World War II, but they came back to a church that had survived the fire of Japanese persecution on its own and had confidence its own leadership. By the time I arrived in Taiwan, in addition to British and Canadian Presbyterian missionaries, there were also Presbyterians from the United States.

In the separate but related histories of the British and Canadian missions, two Presbyterian seminaries had been established, one in Taipei and one in Tainan, in the southern part of the island. Further removed from the center of power in the north, Tainan Theological College had a well-deserved reputation for resisting government attempts—whether Japanese or of the GRC—to intimidate and control it. Taiwan Theological College, in Shih Lin outside Taipei on the road up to Yang Ming Shan, was a more conservative seminary reflecting the theology and political caution of the North Synod.

An appointment of a Methodist missionary to either seminary was not without precedent. When I arrived, a Methodist missionary, Ted Cole, was on the faculty in Tainan. A few years earlier, an arrangement had been in the works for J. Harry Haines, earlier a missionary on the Mainland, to be appointed at the northern seminary to teach church history. The appointment didn't work out because of his election to become general secretary of the Methodist Committee on Relief in New York. Within the first couple of months of my arrival, I was approached by both seminaries and invited to join their faculties. The offers were flattering, but I was mindful of a missionary reality. The seminaries would not have to pay my salary because I was a missionary; they would only have to provide a residence. That notwithstanding, I thought with no lack of presumption that either seminary would be lucky to have me.

The decision was not mine to make, however. The power to place missionaries was in the hands of the area secretary in New York and the resident bishop, a U.S. bishop who was himself (and at the time they were all "him") appointed by the Council of Bishops. The East Asia Area Secretary was responsible for missionaries in Korea, Japan, Taiwan, and Hong Kong. The bishop was assigned to the two provisional annual conferences for the Hong Kong-Taiwan area for a four-year period.

Technically, the bishop had the authority to make any appointment of clergy, but few were made without the approval of the Area Secretary for the board. I made my appeal to both. Margaret Billingsley came out of the missionary experience in Korea and was nearing retirement. In response to my letter to her in which I pointed out how the need for a church history teacher specializing in non-Western church history fit my qualifications, she wrote back,

"Tainan Theological School has asked for every missionary we have. This seems to be their general procedure."

A paragraph later she gave me the news that Don and Helen MacInnis would be leaving Soochow University and said I would be needed there.

"Also, I was hoping that you would teach some at the Theological School in Taipei so that they could have some fresh teaching and ideas brought into the school there," she wrote.

Bishop Hazen Werner agreed with Dr. Billingsley, but he opened the door wider to my teaching in a seminary. In my second year of language study, the two of them would agree on my being based at the northern seminary as well as teaching part time in Tainan, an assignment that worked well both for teaching what I was trained for and was better for what would become my non-seminary activities.

When I arrived in Taiwan, Don Wilson was the Associate General Secretary of the Presbyterian Church of Taiwan, a position usually reserved for a missionary. Don was a tall, slender member of the U.S. United Presbyterian Church serving under the auspices of the Canadian Presbyterians. Although I spoke no Taiwanese, I understood that Don spoke the language and understood the culture so well that when he spoke the language, if Taiwanese couldn't see him, they would think they were hearing a native speaker, a level of proficiency few missionaries achieved. Don had been in Taiwan for ten years, but it was another person who made the contacts outside the church.

In the early 1960s, George Todd of the Urban Ministries program of the United Presbyterian Church came to work for two years in Tainan. Because of his short term, he was not given language training. At his own expense, he hired a Taiwanese companion who went with him everywhere and translated for him. First thing every morning, George had this interpreter read the morning Chinese paper to him. George had been involved in creating the East Harlem Protestant Parish, a pioneering urban ministry in New York City. He was politically conscious with the mind of a community organizer. In his brief time on the island, George made it his business to get to know people at every level of society. That included Taiwanese who had resisted the heavy hand of the Kuomintang, something few other missionaries had dared do. Before he left Taiwan, he passed those contacts on to Don Wilson.

Judith and I had met George at Stony Point before leaving for Taiwan. He talked with us about the ways he had found to move beneath surface appearances and understand often unheard perspectives among the people. He encouraged us to get to know Don Wilson. "He will introduce you to people who can help you gain a fuller understanding," he said.

One afternoon in the late spring, Don called to ask if he could come by. He knew me because of the possibility that I might teach at one of the seminaries, and at a social gathering, we had had a conversation about the situation in Taiwan. After he removed his shoes and exchanged pleasantries, he took time to ooh and ahh over Elizabeth. Then he came to the point of his visit. Judith and he handed Elizabeth to Su-ching and we sat down in the living room.

"You told me you wanted to know more about the political reality here, didn't you?" he asked.

"Yes, we did," I said, relieved that we were about to have a conversation I had been wanting for months.

"Do you know who Dr. Peng Ming-min is?"

"No," I had to confess. Judith was also shaking her head.

"Dr. Peng's grandfather was the first Taiwanese Presbyterian minister on the island. His father was a doctor but is dead. His mother, who lives in Kaohsiung, is active in the church, but Peng has not been."

This was starting out like a church conversation, and I wasn't sure where it was going.

"Peng was educated in Japan during World War II. He lost an arm in an American bombing attack in Nagasaki and was just outside the city a few months later when the atomic bomb was dropped on that city," Don said.

"A brilliant student," he went on, "Peng later studied at McGill University in Canada and received a doctorate from the Sorbonne in Paris before returning to Taiwan in 1954. Peng became one of the most popular lecturers at Tai-Da, the National University in Taipei and head of the Political Science Department. He is said to be the youngest department head in the history of the school—almost unheard of because of his age and because he was Taiwanese. As a specialist in international law, he wrote a paper that laid the basis for space law. When Peng returned to Taiwan, he was at the peak of his career and recognized as a pioneer in space law. He was invited to seminars at Harvard University with Henry Kissinger. He became a part of the Nationalist Chinese delegation to the United Nations. Because the government wanted him to spy on Taiwanese independence groups in the United States, Peng said he began to be uneasy about his association with the Nationalist government."

Don had my full attention.

"Later, Peng would say that the government made a mistake sending him to the United Nations because there he would be politicized and would turn against it."

Don looked at his watch and said he had to get to another appointment.

"But how did he turn against the government? What did he do?" I sputtered.

"Why don't you ask him yourself?" Don said as he stood to leave. "You said you wanted to know about the reality in Taiwan. I know of no one in the world who can help you understand that better than Dr. Peng. Would you like to have dinner with him next Friday night?"

Chapter Eight
Dinner and a Show (of Force)

If you could just see facts flat-on, without that
horrible moral squint... With a little common sense
you could have made a statesman.

— Cardinal Wolsey to Sir Thomas Moore,
— *A Man for All Seasons*

Don sat on the little bench by the door, replacing slippers with his shoes. So tall and thin was he that when he stood up, he looked like a ladder unfolding. Judith and I were trying to recover from the shock of the invitation.

"I'll come by to pick you up," he said as I held the door open for him. "It's probably best if you don't tell anyone else about this." Then he was gone.

At church Sunday, it was hard not telling the McKeels. Judith and I could hardly wait for Friday night.

Don arrived at our gate promptly and held the taxi while we gathered our things and came out. Taxis, most of them Datsuns, were replacing pedicabs. Don folded himself into the front seat while Judith and I got into the back.

"The Pengs live in National University housing about ten minutes from here," he said as the taxi lurched out into the sea of pedestrians, bicycles, pedicabs, and other taxis on the street.

"Does he teach at Tai-Da?" I asked.

"No. The authorities won't allow it," he said. I think he could see the confusion on our faces. "Dr. Peng was released from prison just before you arrived at the end of the year."

"Why was he in prison?"

"I guess I should have told you the other day. He and two of his former students were arrested in 1964 for printing and attempting to circulate a document they called 'A Manifesto for Self-Salvation.' It was a kind of attempt to do what Martin Luther did when he posted his 'Ninety-five Theses' on the door of the Wittenberg Church, except that Luther wanted to provoke a discussion within the Catholic Church while Peng and the others wanted a national debate on the legitimacy of the Chiang government. The government wasn't amused, and under martial law they could have been given death sentences. Peng and his friends received eight- and ten-year sentences. Peng was released but the two students were not."

"Why not?" I asked as the taxi slowed down and stopped in front of a Japanese house with a wall around it much like the one we lived in.

"Dr. Peng was probably released—with this regime one can only guess—because he was so well-known in international academic and government circles that his imprisonment was too much of an embarrassment for the government."

One of the things that Don hadn't tell us was how he had made pastoral visits to Mrs. Peng during the time Dr. Peng was in prison because their Taiwanese friends were too fearful to do so. He also hadn't told us how he continued the visits to both of them after Peng was released, even though a military jeep was parked at the end of his street.

Don paid the driver and we rang the bell at the gate. I noticed a squatter hut outside the wall a few feet away much like the one on the corner near Number 9 and, as I was finding out, all over the city.

A slender man with a broad smile opened the gate and gestured for us to come inside. He introduced us to his wife, who was standing behind him. Both exchanged greetings with Don in Taiwanese and then introduced themselves to Judith and me in English. We removed our shoes and ascended the two steps to the tatami floor of the house.

"So, you are studying Mandarin," Dr. Peng said.

"Yes, that's the policy for Methodist missionaries who work here."

"What will you do when you finish language school?"

"I came to be the chaplain at Soochow, but the position has been filled. I may teach at one of the Presbyterian seminaries."

"We're doing our best to convince the Methodists," Don said.

"What would you teach?" Dr. Peng asked.

"My field is the history of Christianity in the non-Western world. I would probably teach church history," I said. "And Judith plans to teach English."

There was such a sense of ease and lack of pretension in the man that I had difficulty believing that he was only recently out of prison.

"I understand your field is political science, but the government won't allow you to teach," I said.

"It is true. I guess they are afraid that I might contaminate the minds of students with treasonous thoughts," he said. "Since they won't let me teach here, I've requested permission to go abroad, but they won't allow that, either. I guess they are worried about those students too," he said with a laugh.

"You did have quite an influence on at least two of your students, the ones who were with you in writing the document that landed you all in prison."

"Wei and Hsieh were very good students," he said as his smile momentarily disappeared. I imagined his thinking of them still in prison when he was not. The smile reappeared and he said, "They didn't need me to get in trouble with the government. We did it together.

"Both were graduates from the law school. Hsieh Tsung-ming is the son of a wealthy family in central Taiwan. Although not finishing at the top of his class, he presented an outstanding thesis on constitutional law. Wei Ting-chao was 'Hakka,' the son of a farmer. Wei had been a good student in law school but upon graduation chose to work in a coal mine for several months so he could 'gain experience of real life.' Then, he took a job as a research assistant at the prestigious Academia Sinica.

"We spent many hours in the evenings in this room talking about the illegitimacy of the present regime. Instead of fearing what the secret police might hear, we thought that the people of Taiwan should be discussing important questions publicly. What is the 'government of China,' which has lost China forever? Whom does it represent? How long is one going to continue to accept the fiction of Nationalist government as 'government of China' and the myth of 'recovery of Mainland China by this government?'

"We got tired of talking and decided to do something. We wrote what is translated in English as a 'Manifesto for Formosan Self-Salvation'."

"What did you hope to achieve?" I asked.

I suspect that Mrs. Peng knew that his answer would take a while, so before he had a chance to answer, she invited us to the table.

"We wanted to affirm that return to the Mainland is absolutely impossible," Peng continued once the conversation resumed, "and by unifying the island population, regardless of place of origin, to bring about the overthrow of the Chiang regime, establishing a new country and a new government. We wanted to have the constitution rewritten, guaranteeing basic human rights and obtaining true democracy by establishing an efficient administration responsible to the people. We want to participate in the UN as a new member, establishing diplomatic relations with other countries striving together for world peace. We did not think this unreasonable if the people were given an opportunity to discuss the issues openly.

"We found a printer who we thought we could trust. He printed ten thousand copies. We took them by pedicab to a hotel room in Manka, which was our base of operations. Manka is one of the oldest and most disreputable sections of Taipei, and the hotel was one that usually rented its rooms by the hour. Quite suitable for our project, don't you think?" he said, smiling.

"Hsieh had taken the completed copies by pedicab to the apartment of a university student who didn't ask any questions about what she was storing. The next step was to prepare address labels and mail them to Taiwanese all over the island.

"We didn't get to make the labels. There was a loud banging on the door. Before we could open it, eight plainclothes police, revolvers in hand, burst into the room and arrested us. As the room was searched— we knew this would be the last time we would see each other before trial and after that not for years—we agreed that we would simply tell the truth about what we had done."

Peng grew silent as if lost in thought. No one else spoke.

"We weren't members of organized crime, which is said to run Manka, or revolutionaries. We were campus intellectuals undone by our underestimation of the police state against which we were protesting," Peng said.

His striking candor and lack of pretense continued throughout the evening as we left the table and returned to the living room with the conversation shifting from the arrest and imprisonment to the political situation in Taiwan. We even talked about the Cultural Revolution and the fear it was generating in the United States.

"Most Taiwanese are not interested in communism. There are persons accused of being Communists in prison here, but nearly all of them are Mainlanders. Most are falsely accused. For the Taiwanese, our distrust of Mainland Chinese is primary. We distrust Mainlanders as much as Marxist ideology. Most Taiwanese will tell you, 'We don't want Chiang and we don't want Mao.'"

At eleven o'clock, the party began to break up. Before we could leave, Don shocked us by saying that in June he and his family were going on furlough. He doubted that the government would allow him to return. He said the words and it hit me: Don had arranged the evening in the hope that the contact with Dr. Peng passed by George Todd to him would now be maintained by us if he were unable to return in September.

We persuaded Don that we could hail a cab and get back home on our own. He was still there when we left. As Dr. Peng watched us to the gate, my mind went to the American Academy Awards Best Picture film of 1966, *A Man for All Seasons*. Robert Bolt's play, on which the film is based, is about Sir Thomas Moore in sixteenth-century England, the true story of one man's refusal to swerve from his spiritual and intellectual convictions even at the insistence of King Henry III. It was a play about conscious and a steadfast heart. I saw the movie before leaving for Taiwan. As he bid us good night, I felt I was shaking the hand of another Sir Thomas Moore.

We hailed a taxi, got into the back seat of the little Datsun, and started down the street. Perhaps a little nervous after what we had heard, one of us looked out the back of the window to see a man who had been walking along in front of the house suddenly break into a run and go around a corner. Within seconds, a military jeep came from around the corner as if it had been shot from a gun.

"We can't go home," we said to each other. "They will follow us."

We told the driver to take us to the East Gate district downtown, far away from Chi Nan Road and home. We thought we might lose the jeep or at least be able to get out and get lost in the crowd in the movie district. The jeep roared right up onto the tail of our cab, the bright lights almost blinding us and the driver. I don't know what the driver was thinking; we didn't say anything to him, except where to take us. For a couple of miles the jeep rode our tail. We could have been stopped, but weren't. That was some comfort because at first we thought the jeep might just run over us.

Our hope to get lost in the movie crowds was dashed when we arrived and found the movie district deserted. All we could see open was a coffee house. We paid the driver before he stopped, jumped out, and hurried inside. The cab sped away, but the jeep stopped just short of the coffee house. We went inside and upstairs to a balcony from where we could see the street. Terrified at the prospect of whoever was in the large jeep coming through the door and grabbing us, we ordered coffee and tried to talk rationally about what had happened and what to do next. There was no one we dared call. What would Don or Dr. Peng do? Finally, the jeep left. We waited until after midnight. It looked as if the coffee shop was about to close. In any event, we didn't want to be the last customers out. We stepped out onto the street and wondered if we could find a cab or if the sinister jeep would reappear and run us down.

Fortunately for us, several taxis came around the circle and we hailed one. We watched through the back window, but it didn't appear that anyone was following us.

We were relieved to get back to Number 9 and find Elizabeth sound asleep in her crib. Su-ching woke up and reported that the evening had been uneventful. The adrenalin rush over the last couple of hours increased our weariness but prevented sleep from coming easily. We had said we wanted to find out about the political reality in Taiwan. We had our first lesson.

Chapter Nine
If They Only Knew

We must always take sides. Neutrality helps the oppressor, never the victim. Silence encourages the tormentor, never the tormented.

— Eli Wiesel (1928-)

While we had been thoroughly frightened, we were not deterred from seeing Peng again. Before we left that evening, we had invited him to come see us, and he assured us he would. A day or two later in the late afternoon, we received a phone call. "I can be there in fifteen or twenty minutes. Are you sure it is convenient?"

"Of course, we are anxious to see you. Can you stay for dinner?"

"Oh no, I don't want to impose on you. Maybe I should come another time."

"Please come. It won't be like at your house the other night. This is our amah's night off and we are having leftovers, but there are plenty of those," I said, not considering what cultural faux pas we might be committing by such an invitation to eat leftovers. In discussing it later, Judith and I sensed that with this man it would be okay.

"We are anxious to see you. Can Mrs. Peng come? She would also be welcome." Extending the leftover invitation to Mrs. Peng was stretching the limits of even a westerner's informality, but I felt it would have been more impolite not to invite her at all.

"No, she will not be able to come. I will explain when I see you. I will be there in a few minutes."

To say that we were anxious to see Peng was a considerable understatement. We wanted to know if he knew anything about what happened after we left his house. Don had gone south and we had been unable to talk with him. We had both been captivated by Dr. Peng.

Knowing who he was had something to do with the attraction, but his seeming openness to us made us want to get to know him better.

"Oh, I am so sorry you had to go through that," he said as we ate and explained what happened on Friday night. "I didn't know."

"From your description of the jeep, it sounds like it was the Garrison Command, one of several secret police agencies of the regime, and headed by Chiang Ching-kuo, son of the Generalissimo."

"Do you think they have been watching your house?" I asked, prompting a chuckle from Peng.

"Don may not have known that I am under watch twenty-four hours a day. They use the little squatter's house outside my gate as their post. When I come out, one or two men follow me wherever I go," he said.

"Did they follow you today?" I said, wondering if they were waiting outside.

"Oh, no," he said. "Although they are not supposed to, the guards go to sleep at night. I go out after midnight and they never know I'm gone."

"Have you been out since last night?" I asked.

"Yes, I will go home before five in the morning and they'll think I've been in the house for the last twenty-four hours."

We spent the evening talking about politics, our families, and the culture. I even confessed my uneasiness about inviting a guest to eat leftovers.

"Your invitation means that you did not treat me as a guest, but as a friend," he responded.

Peng became a regular visitor at our house, albeit sometimes at strange hours. He visited us on an average of once a week for the next four years. While the different secret police and security agencies would find out about a lot about our activities, there has never been any indication that the Nationalists or the U.S. government ever learned of these visits. Had they known, I'm sure that our sojourn in Taiwan would have been much shorter.

Peng, it seemed to us, was a lonely man. At first we simply became friends. He seemed to enjoy our company as we did his. He was also grieving because Hsieh and Wei were in prison and he was not. But at the same time, he was creating a communication network among like-minded Taiwanese around the island.

"Would you be willing to help?" Peng asked one day after another one of our long conversations about the problems in Taiwan.

"There are things we could do that if done by us would likely result only in our deportation, but if done by the Taiwanese could cost their lives." I said, not as a question but a conclusion we had already drawn.

"Because this regime is brutal and unpredictable, you can't be sure of what they might do to you," Peng replied, "but you are right that, whatever the case, the risk to you would be less than that to a Taiwanese."

In a flash, I remembered all of the warnings about how missionaries should not become "politically involved," a message regularly sounded in the Methodist missionary community. Those who gave such warnings did not consider their kowtowing to the Generalissimo and Madame Chiang as political involvement.

The more I thought about it, the more embarrassed I was for the missionary community and my identification with it. Since my graduate work had involved the history of Christian missions, I should not have been surprised at what I found in the Methodist mission in Taiwan. While the history of missions contains many noble exceptions, by and large missions and missionaries either acquiesced to the colonial policies that made their presence possible or actively supported them. While it might be pointed out that the Republic of China was not a "colony" of the United States, the Methodist mission, of which I was a part, turned a blind eye to what was happening on the island and curried the favor of both the ROC and the U.S. in order to retain its position on the island. The difference to me seemed semantic and not substantive.

I was surprised to discover that the problem was not limited to missionaries. I discovered that Dick and Leigh Kagan were also embarrassed that more of their fellow graduate students in Chinese studies from universities in the U.S. studying in Taiwan were not more concerned about the political situation.

We met Dick and Leigh out on the street in front of our house as we each pushed our babies in strollers. They lived at Number 20, a few doors down the street from us. Both of them were in Taiwan on fellowships—Leigh from Harvard and Dick from the University of Pennsylvania. Their little girl, Rachel, was eight months older than Elizabeth.

Graduate students came to Taiwan to work in many different fields of Chinese studies. The Mainland was closed and Taiwan was the best place not only for Mandarin language studies but also many Chinese classics and other historical documents. Dick and Leigh helped us understand how graduate students coming to Taiwan were warned not to get politically involved. After all, they were told, they needed to get their studies done, and they shouldn't do anything to make it more difficult for students from their university to come after them. We understood that the great China scholar at Harvard, John King Fairbanks, was especially emphatic on the point.

It seemed curious to me that these graduate students and professors with extensive backgrounds in Chinese studies could choose to ignore what was happening under their noses or justify their silence to maintain their access to the island. The Kagans said that university professors in the U.S. were reluctant to publish articles critical of the Nationalist government in order to keep the doors open for their students to continue coming to Taiwan. It was the same song the missionaries sang, except without a "university" verse.

One of the refreshing things about the Kagans was that they were also embarrassed by that reality and had already taken some risks. He had done a master's in East Asian history at the University of California at Berkley and had gone on to the University of Pennsylvania to work on his doctorate. There he had become active in a small group of scholars who opposed American foreign policy in East Asia, especially Saigon, Seoul, and Taipei. In Taiwan, he sought out and interviewed dissident leaders.

Dick was a Jewish conscientious objector. His Jewish heritage informed his sense of justice. I found myself fantasizing about converting to Judaism, where somehow there seemed to be more integrity. But it was only a fantasy. Had there been a Jewish community in Taipei, I suspect its members would have compromised their sense of justice as much as the missionaries and the graduate students. Although Dick and Leigh left at the end of our first year, they helped us think through the issues around involvement in politics. They encouraged us in the decisions we were about to make. They vowed to assist us once back in the States, and they did.

"As we see it," I said because Judith and I had already talked the issue through with the Kagans and agreed, "we don't have the option of not being involved in some way. It is not simply a matter of being politically involved in a host country; our State Department is already involved here propping up this government. If we do nothing, we are putting our stamp of approval of what our State Department is doing here."

"In good conscience, we can't do that," added Judith, "so the answer to your question is yes, we will do what we can."

The only important question that remained was what could we do and how we could do it.

The first thing we thought was important for us was to provide accurate information for people who visited Taiwan.

"If people in the U.S. knew what our government was supporting here in Taiwan, it would be harder to perpetuate the 'Free China' myth," I said to Dr. Peng on one of his visits.

Not ten years had passed since Senator Joe McCarthy's paranoid assault on the fears of communism in the U.S. Also, word of the horrors of the Cultural Revolution were beginning to leak out of Mao's China while the U.S.'s involvement in Vietnam was rapidly expanding. In the midst of such developments, perhaps it was unrealistic to try and convince Americans that Taiwan was neither "free" nor "China," as we had come to see.

We had found Peng to be so approachable and credible that we thought one small contribution we could make was to arrange meetings for him with visitors from outside the island. One of the expectations of missionaries was to entertain visitors, many of whom were contributors to the Taiwanese mission in their churches back in the States. What was expected was that we would show them "the work," meaning the Methodist mission work. That responsibility was borne primarily by missionaries assigned to be "port hosts," but we were all expected to help when we could.

Some visitors were more interested in shopping than seeing "the work" or knowing about life in Taiwan, but we were surprised at the number who seemed genuinely interested in what was really happening on the island. We shared our perspective with them, even to the point of alarming some of our missionary colleagues, who thought it inappropriate to talk about such things at all, even if they knew them to be true.

If the visitors seemed serious, we would arrange a meeting with Dr. Peng. The meetings had to be secret. Sometimes we arranged for them to meet him at our home, but more often at a restaurant. He would make sure he was not followed and we would make sure we were not followed. Over dinner, Peng would share his perspective in a calm tone, patiently answering the most basic questions. Although the visitors were most always impressed, we soon came to believe that most of these people didn't know enough about the realities of Taiwan to take advantage of the opportunity they had in a conversation with Peng.

We decided that if we had print resources we could put in the hands of visitors beforehand, meetings with Peng would be much more fruitful and more worthy of his time and the risk we all took in arranging the meetings. We did not want revolutionary tracts; we wanted articles that would be credible to scholars and understandable to laypeople. Of course, under martial law, which had been in effect since 1949, possession of such documents was a serious offense. Since the articles would have to be published anonymously, they had to be credible on their own. We tried to explain that in the foreword:

We are a group of men and women of local and foreign nationalities residing in Formosa (Taiwan) whose professions comprise the fields of religion, education and public affairs. Our primary purpose in compiling this paper is to point out some issues that should provoke thoughtful discussion of the realities in this country. While we are aware of the disadvantages of remaining anonymous, we choose to do so both for the sake of our own safety and for that of our families and friends. That such secrecy is necessary is, in itself, indicative of the nature of the regime by which this island is governed.

We know that a vast amount of public funds and great official efforts are being expended abroad by the Chinese Nationalist Government to maintain an image of this country as a worthy member of the "free and democratic" world. We know also that abundant official publications boasting of the Kuomintang's (Nationalist Party) achievement in Formosa are being distributed to foreign visitors here. Thus we feel acutely a need to present a more balanced picture to those who are concerned with what the real situation in Formosa might be. With these things in mind, we have compiled several articles – some previously published – which are at considerable variance with the governmental propaganda and which, we feel, as a result of our own observations and personal experiences, reflect more truthfully the actual situation in Formosa under Chinese Nationalist rule. Emphasis is given to the political situation because we are convinced that this political situation affects the whole of life here – partly by making impossible any changes in the present structures that might contribute to the realization of social justice – and that any discussion of the problems in Formosa is superficial unless this basic political problem is recognized.

How would we get articles to give to foreign visitors? We would produce them—summarize important books, copy articles from journals, and write some articles ourselves.

Where was one to begin in explaining to foreign visitors that what they had been taught to believe was "Free China" was, in the view of many, if not most, Taiwanese neither "Free" nor "China"? The American public was largely ignorant of the "current events" in Taiwan since World War II, not to mention the history of the island before that. In our minds, the beginning point of conversation about a Taiwanese perspective was "2-28," referring to February 28, 1947, a date etched into the hearts and minds of Taiwanese people like Pearl Harbor had been for Americans six years earlier. On that day, an incident took place in Taipei that led to the massive slaughter of thousands of Taiwanese at the hands of Chiang Kai-shek's Chinese troops. The event was the beginning of repressive martial law on the island, or what came to be called the "White Terror."

While most Taiwanese knew about Pearl Harbor within days of the event, it was safe to say that few Americans knew anything about 2-28. While Tillman and Peggy Durdin wrote about reports of the massacre from Nanking and posted them in the *New York Times* and *The Nation*,[12] the attention of war-weary people in the U.S. was on the descending Iron Curtain in Europe.

A young American diplomat, George H. Kerr, affiliated with the U.S. Consulate in Taipei at the time of the massacre, witnessed many of the atrocities. His book,

---

[12] Tillman Durdin, "Formosa Killings Are Put at 10,000," *New York Times*, March 29, 1947; Peggy Durdin, "Terror in Taiwan," *The Nation*, March 24, 1947 (http://www.taiwandc.org/hst-1947.htm).

Formosa Betrayed[13], published in 1965, provided the first glimpse many Americans had of the horrors of 2-28. Kerr not only described in great detail the events leading up to and through the 2-28 massacre, he also documented the U.S. military blueprint of the undefined status of Taiwan in the 1951 peace treaty with Japan.

Two years later, Chen Lung-Chu and Harold D. Lasswell published an analysis of the international status of Taiwan, *Formosa, China, and the United Nations: Formosa in the World Community[14]*. They had impressive credentials. Chen was a senior research fellow in international law and international human rights at Yale; Lasswell was a professor of law and political science at Yale. They began with how the island had been ceded to Japan at the end of the Sino-Japanese War in 1895. At the end of World War II, Japan surrendered Taiwan to Chiang Kai-shek acting on behalf of the United States and other Allied powers. Immediately after suppressing the 2-28 incident, the Nationalist government unilaterally claimed Formosa a regular province of China. As the Nationalists continued to lose the civil war on the Mainland, most observers felt it was simply a matter of time before the Nationalist regime would be exterminated. The outbreak of the Korean War in 1950 changed that. President Truman, while proclaiming the "neutralization of Formosa" and dispatching the United Seventh Fleet to prevent any attack on Formosa and any operations launched from there on the Mainland, stated that "the determination of the future status of Formosa must await the restoration of security in the Pacific, a peace settlement with Japan, or consideration by the United Nations." In the peace treaty with Japan, signed in September of 1951, Japan formally renounced "all right, title, and claim to Formosa and the Pescadores." Formosa was "detached" from Japan but was

---

[13] George H. Kerr, *Formosa Betrayed* (New York: Houghton-Mifflin Company, 1965).
[14] Lung-chu Chen, Harold D. Lasswell, *Formosa, China, and the United Nations : Formosa in the world community* (New York: St. Martin's Press, 1967).

not "attached" to anyone since the treaty didn't specify any beneficiary of Japan's renunciation.

As things stood in 1967, when the book was published, the Chinese Nationalists had both effective control over Taiwan and the China seat in the United Nations. Although outside the framework of the United Nations, the People's Republic of China claimed Taiwan and the Nationalist seat in the UN. Chen and Lasswell argued that the overwhelming majority of Formosans abhorred both the Nationalist and Communist regimes and hoped to achieve independence through self-determination. The authors argued for a "One China, One Formosa" solution.

These two books had begun to fill a void in academic perspectives that for years had taken only Nationalist and Communist claims into account. We thought foreigners ought to know about these two books, so Dr. Peng wrote twelve-page condensations of each of them for the packet.

Together, we selected other articles for inclusion in the clandestine packet:

"The Majority Problem in Formosa," an article that appeared in *Student World*, a World Student Christian Federation publication;

"General Wedemeyer on the Nationalist Occupation of Formosa," excerpted from *United States Relations with China,*;

"Formosa: Solidarity of Gloom," by Marilyn Blatt Young;

"Taiwan – DISNEYLAND EAST," by Arnold Abrams;

"The China Impasse: A Formosan View," by Li Thian-hok;

"Chiang Kai-Shek's Silent Enemies," by Albert Axelbank,; and

"Government Influence on Education in Taiwan Today," an original article written by one of our academic friends.

After we selected the pieces we wanted and wrote the foreword, we decided that we needed an introductory article, one that would point to the rest and provide an overview for the people who read only one article. Peng could have done exactly what was needed, but we didn't want him writing anything that could be traced to him. So we turned to one of our academic writer friends who agreed to write the article for us. It's called "An Introduction" and it is well-written, as one might expect of a writer for the *New York Times.*

Back in the States, the Kagans told Fox Butterfield to get acquainted with us when he came to Taiwan. Fox was a graduate student from Harvard and a stringer for the *New York Times.* He had been born with a silver academic spoon in his mouth. His father was the famous Harvard scholar who edited The Adams Papers. Fox was always interested in getting a story for the *Times,* but we found that we both liked and could trust each other. His occasional stories in the *Times* were good—better than most of the other news stories published about Taiwan.

Later Fox would become the *Times* bureau chief in Saigon, Tokyo, Hong Kong, Beijing, and Boston and a correspondent in Washington and New York. He would win the Pulitzer Prize as a member of the *New York Times* team that published the Pentagon Papers, a secret government study of decision-making about the Vietnam War leaked to the newspaper. It prepared a series of lengthy articles and published them in 1971.

One of the things that impressed us in 1966 was Fox's journalistic integrity. When asked about his craft, he would reply, "I was trained to think you've got to write what you find, warts and all, if you believe it to be accurate."

That's what we wanted—someone who would write about Taiwan, "warts and all." We unimaginatively titled his article "An Introduction." It was that and it lead the reader to the other articles. But it was more than an introduction. We might have better named it "What Americans Should Look for in Taiwan—And What They Should Ask Themselves."

What we had to ask ourselves, he said, was what role our government was playing in Taiwan. Despite State Department officers' bland pronouncements that they did not interfere in "China's domestic affairs," Fox pointed out that the U.S. propping up the Chiang government was intervention, as was training Ching-kuo's secret police and providing them with the latest equipment. He closed with the words of the editor of a magazine shut down by the government:

> America is basically hypocritical. You hold up Chiang Kai-shek when he would fall down by himself; but you say there is nothing you can do to improve the political situation. Don't you care about democracy?

Selection, writing, and editing the pieces for the packet, although time consuming, was the easiest part of the project. Getting them printed and distributed were different matters altogether.

Chapter Ten
Word Spreads

*What gunpowder did for war the printing press has
done for the mind.*

— Abolitionist Wendell Phillips (1811-1884)

Before we decided on anything, we made several
decisions. The first was about risk assessment. We knew
if and when we got into trouble with the authorities that
any Taiwanese with whom we were working would in all
likelihood suffer far worse consequences than we would.
We assumed the worst that would happen to us was
deportation. There would be times later when I wondered
if we had been right about that assumption. We would be
right about how much more Taiwanese associated with us
would suffer. Because of the differing levels of risk, we
decided that we would only be involved in antigovernment
activity with Taiwanese who knew the risks and who had
already been in prison. Peng, and later Hsieh and Wei, all
knew the probable consequences of our activities far better
than we green Americans did.

While that first decision limited the number persons
with which we would be involved, it also made clear with
whom we would not be involved. Before our appointments
to the seminary had been made, we decided that we would
not let our students or Taiwanese faculty know what we
were doing with Peng and others. In some cases, students
and faculty would come to know something of how we felt
about the Taiwanese situation, but as far as they were
concerned, it was just how we felt.

We involved other foreigners. Since we always operated
on a need-to-know basis, few of the missionary colleagues,
foreign graduate students, or U.S. government employees
we recruited to help ever knew about the things we were
doing in which they were not directly involved. We tried to

arrange at least one meeting with Peng for them as individuals or couples so that they could hear him make his case. We only approached missionary colleagues we knew shared our general view of the situation. Not surprisingly, most of those had been through the Stony Point missionary orientation.

One of the other decisions we made at the outset was that we would not engage in any public protest, choosing rather to work quietly and secretly to prolong giving the government any reason to kick us out as much as we could. We couldn't imagine any public protest we might make that would aid the cause anyway.

The first of our projects, which we dubbed "Educating Americans," was directed only at foreigners and would continue as long as we were in Taiwan. We weren't out to change Taiwanese views. That, I believed, would have been irresponsible "political involvement" for American citizens. We were, however, out to change American views, a kind of involvement in politics that we believed to be our responsibility as citizens, especially given the kind of information to which we now had access. One-party rule by the Kuomintang, their multiple secret police agencies, and their stacked courts cared nothing about what might be citizen involvement in another country or even the provisions of the ROC constitution. Under martial law, dissent was not tolerated.

After Peng, Hsieh, and Wei printed and almost got their manifesto distributed in 1964, the government tried to make unauthorized printing more difficult. Not only were all printing presses registered with the government, but mimeograph machines as well. How were we to get our selection of articles printed?

Wayne and Jane McKeel were the first foreigners we recruited to help. Because Wayne was a State Department employee, they had access to the U.S. Military PX. They not only agreed to purchase the machine from the PX—where it would not have to be registered with the ROC government —they also paid the two hundred dollars for it themselves and donated it to our cause. They also bought the paper at the same place and contributed that as well. Jane helped us type the stencils.

As far as we know, the first time these papers got into the hands of a U.S. intelligence agency was in Tainan, three hundred miles south of Taipei. In early 1967, while I was still in language school, Bishop Werner and Dr. Billingsley agreed that I would be appointed as associate professor of church history at Taiwan Theological College just outside Taipei and visiting professor at Tainan Theological College in the south. Once a month, I would ride the "tourist train" for the six- or seven-hour trip to Tainan, where I would spend a couple of days teaching specially scheduled classes.

These monthly trips allowed me to maintain contact with some missionary colleagues we had recruited for our project—Sid and Judy Hormell and Rowland and Judy Van Es. They both had a few sets of the papers and were to distribute them to interested foreigners as they saw fit. Their explanation about the source of the papers, like ours, was that they didn't know who produced them.

Sid was in his early thirties and slightly balding. He had a Ph.D. in mass communication from the University of Illinois and was teaching mass communication at the seminary. He had once been a radio announcer in Sitka, Alaska. He had also done a Howdy Doody-style children's radio program. Sid loved to embellish his stories, usually acting them out as he told them. He was also one of the brightest people I have ever known.

At a Christmas party for Americans—from the government, military, church, and private sector—Sid got into a conversation with a person he thought was a civilian. The conversation led to talk about the "situation in Taiwan." The man appeared quite interested, so Sid decided to give the man a set of the papers.

Later that night, there was a knock on Sid and Judy's door at the seminary. Wearing his bathrobe, Sid opened the door and saw the man to whom he had given the papers. Another man was standing behind him.

The men identified themselves as U.S. military intelligence. Telling the story to me later, he swore that the two men really wore trench coats and hats just like in the movies.

"We're sorry to bother you this late at night, and we wouldn't if it were not important. Where did you get the papers you gave me tonight?"

"I told you at the party. They were given me by a tourist who visited the seminary," Sid said.

"You don't remember the name of the person?"

"No. It was at a social gathering here at the seminary. I had never met him before."

"I don't think you are telling us the truth," said the second man. "You could get into serious trouble for lying to us."

"Look, guys," Sid said, waving his hands as he always did when he talked, "why wouldn't I tell you the truth? We're on the same side, you know."

The questioning continued with the same questions and the same answers. Getting nowhere, they left.

A couple of days later Sid received a call from the commander of the U.S. air base near Tainan. Sid had preached a time or two at the base chapel and had met the commander.

"Could you come out to the base this afternoon?" the commander asked. Before Sid could respond, he added "I've taken the liberty of sending a car for you so you won't have to take a taxi."

"I guess so," Sid stammered, "but I have to be back for a class at three o'clock."

"You'll be back in plenty of time," the commander said and hung up.

The car dropped Sid off at the base in front of the building that housed the commander's office.

"I'm here to see the commander," he said

"There must be some mistake," the secretary said after checking the appointment book in front of her. "I do not see an appointment for you."

"That's probably because he just called me to come half an hour ago," Sid said.

The secretary picked up the phone and asked someone about the appointment.

"I'm sorry," she said. "The commander is tied up until four o'clock."

"I've got to get back to the seminary for my class," Sid muttered as he went out the door. Going down the hall toward the exit, a side door opened and the commander himself reached out and pulled Sid into his office. He sat Sid down on a chair in the middle of the room, turned on a radio in the corner, and sat down on another chair almost knee to knee with Sid.

"I thought you would like to know what they've learned about the papers you gave one of our men the other night," he said in a near whisper.

"The documents were sent to Washington for appraisal. We were afraid that they were being produced here on the island. We don't need that kind of trouble. The good news is that Washington has determined that the papers were from the United States," he said, "printed on a U.S. mimeograph machine and on U.S. paper."

"Really?" Sid said.

"In all likelihood, they were produced by a Taiwanese independence group in the States. I thought you would want to know this," the commander said, smiling.

The two exchanged pleasantries for a few minutes and then Sid was excused through the same side door.

"Was this for real," Sid asked Rowland and me the next time I was in Tainan, "or was it just what they wanted me to think?"

I didn't know what to say. Later experience with U.S. intelligence agency personnel led us not to automatically assume "intelligence." The dress and demeanor of the agents who turned up at our friend's door and the behavior of the commander would have been comical if they hadn't scared us. Assuming he was being watched by his own government's agents, Sid got rid of the other sets he had and didn't give out anymore.

Like the incident after dinner at Dr. Peng's house, Sid's encounter meant that, like a burning match between the toes of an elephant, we had touched powerful forces and they had responded. A review of our operating procedures resulted in three decisions.

First, while we would all take greater care with whom we gave packets to, we wouldn't stop. We didn't want the packets to get into the hands of Chiang's security agencies or those of the U.S., but we knew it was bound to happen. It was up to the four or five people who had packets to decide whom to give them to and then, like Sid, to be ignorant if caught.

Second, we needed a secure way to get send and receive international mail. A former colleague at Stony Point now appointed for work in Hong Kong, Bud Carroll, agreed to set up a post office box there. Because his work put him in regular contact with people coming from and going to Taiwan, he chose foreigners he thought reliable and asked them to hand deliver mail to us. We asked foreigners to take mail out and mail it in Hong Kong or Japan. We and Dr. Peng (and later Wei and Hsieh) had contact with the outside world that didn't go through the postal security system set up by the Kuomintang government. Our route wasn't without risks, but had far fewer than the regular system had.

The third thing we did was give Dr. Peng an English name so that we would not refer to him by his real name at home or with involved colleagues. Our encounters with government agencies suggested that the time might come when even our home would be bugged. Dr. Peng agreed. I'm not sure why we suggested the name "Peter." With Christian backgrounds and training in theology, we knew that Peter had been the name of the head of Jesus' disciples and had been derived from the Aramaic word *cephas*, meaning "rock." That might or might not have been a consideration. Peng agreed to the name, and from that time until now, Peng has been Peter to us.

Chapter Eleven
Somebody Listens

*Hope has two lovely daughters, Anger and
Courage: Anger at what is, but must not be; and
Courage, so that what must be, will be.*

—Augustine (354-430)

"Aren't you dangerously close to committing hubris?"
asked a blond graduate student in Chinese studies that
Fox Butterfield had invited to his apartment with some
other American graduate students to discuss our project.

"The idea that you can actually change people's minds
with these articles..." her voice trailed off without finishing
the sentence, presumably leaving us to see the futility of
such an enterprise.

She had a point. Who did we think we were? We were
a couple of people who until a year or two before knew little
of Taiwan's sordid past and present. Almost by chance we
had developed a close friendship with Dr. Peng. It had been
from him and from Taiwanese and Mainlander dissidents
to whom he had introduced us of a reality that, save for the
aftermath of dinner at his home and the experience of Sid
in Tainan, we could only try to imagine. We certainly were
idealistic and naïve, but the evening was an exercise in
shedding my naiveté in believing that if Americans only
knew, they would want to be involved, at least among this
group of budding East Asian scholars. Both we and Peter
had been excited beforehand about the meeting because
we were meeting with graduate students, presumably
fluent in Chinese and knowledgeable about the situation in
Taiwan. We left aware that we weren't going to receive any
help from them and only hopeful that the risk we took in
bringing Peter to the meeting wouldn't come back to bite
us.

"The young woman's statement," Peter assured us afterward, "was her rationalization for not getting involved. I think you will find that for many 'scholars,' our history and culture are simply objects to study and mean getting a degree and a career in the field. They see themselves as 'objective observers' with no moral or political responsibility for what they learn."

We had already heard this from the Kagans, but it was something else to hear it from someone who had been at the peak of academia. The view Peter characterized appeared to be the polar opposite of the "missionary view" that missionaries came believing that they had the Truth and were coming to deliver it to the unsaved of the island. Both parties, it seemed to me, came with their own sense of cultural superiority and moral irresponsibility.

Once we began distributing the materials, we often didn't fare any better than with the graduate students. After all the trouble and risk we took to print the collection of articles, we found that many of the people didn't take time to read them. Who could blame them? Most were on vacations or business trips and were more interested in shopping and seeing the sights than in spending intellectual energy on understanding a different view of the reality in Taiwan.

Some, we discovered, had such commitments to the Cold War mentality that they had difficulty understanding how any power that was anticommunist could be criticized. The emotions of such folks were exacerbated by the growing U.S. involvement in Vietnam and the polarizing of opinion in the U.S. around that involvement.

While it is true that in Taiwan we were somewhat removed from the ever-enlarging currents of conflict swirling in the United States, we were being politicized by not unrelated events in Taiwan. Wei T'ing-Chao and Hsieh Tsung-Min were nothing if not resourceful. From prison they found ways to get information out to Peter. They began to send Peter lists of political prisoners somehow smuggled out of prison on extremely thin parchment. In a party as corrupt as the KMT, there were always holes in the security system. Dispirited Mainlander soldiers who didn't want to be in Taiwan any more than the Taiwanese people wanted them there opened many of those holes, not because they sympathized with the Taiwanese but because they just didn't care. However they managed it, Wei and Hsieh began to get out regular reports on who was inside and on what charges.

With actual names of prisoners, their locations, and what they were charged with, Peter used our new communications system through Hong Kong to make contact with Amnesty International and give the names to them. To get on one of the published lists and have them inquire about a particular prisoner, Amnesty International wanted assurance that the prisoner was indeed a political prisoner and was not jailed because of violent actions. Peter remembered that just being remembered and having a member of AI write to him while he was in jail boosted his spirits. While it was impossible for someone like Peter to be made to disappear forever from prison, the same was not true for hundreds or thousands of other political prisoners. Being on Amnesty International lists, which were published around the world, was one small lever to keep some of the prisoners alive.

Although what Wei and Hsieh were able to learn about political prisoners in other prisons was nothing short of remarkable, they admitted they had no idea how many prisoners there were on the island. Years later as a legislator, Hsieh would do a study of the White Terror period from 1949 to 1987, the longest period of sustained martial law in world history, he would conclude. In that time 29,407 cases were brought to the martial courts, involving over 140,000 people, with 3,000 to 4,000 being executed. These, he pointed out, did not include those who were murdered by the government outside the judicial system, those who committed suicide to escape torture, or the ones who were warehoused in psychiatric hospitals.

While in 1967 we had no idea of the extent of the White Terror, we rightly suspected that it was far beyond the numbers we were uncovering. All of us knew someone who had a friend or family member disappear without a trace. While he was writing the introductory article for the packet, a friend of Fox disappeared:

> A friend whom I shall call Chang used to remark over the dinner table: "The KMT is a peculiar combination of Fascism, Communism, and traditional despotism, with Chiang Kai-shek the Emperor. Our government isn't any more democratic than the Manchus were 100 years ago. One out of five people on Taiwan is probably a paid police informer." Chang's chances under this system were poor. And then finally last month Chang disappeared. At first his family hoped he might have gone to visit a friend in the countryside, but after two weeks they gave up. Chang, a big rather chubby young Mainlander, was bright and articulate. He had unorthodox ideas on how to improve Taiwan. Like many people who dare to express such ideas, even in private, he has probably been taken to one of the political prisons and will never be heard from again.

One did not have to criticize the government to disappear. The reasons were as capricious as absolute power invites. Hsieh told the story of Liu Ming, a local industrialist who was a benefactor of cultural groups. His crime was owning a luxury Ford sedan, of which there were only two on the island, that was desired by a particular government official. One of Mr. Liu's staff was tortured into confessing that he was a Communist spy, and then Liu was accused of harboring an enemy of the KMT. Liu was not only taken to Green Island, where he was tortured repeatedly, but the KMT also took his property, and his family was left destitute.

The fate of Liu's family was not unique. In a practice that combined the old Chinese "bao jia" system and the Stalinist-structured secret police agencies of the KMT, these families were systematically cut off from financial help—e.g., relatives who acted to help them were visited by special police and warned not to help. They weren't jailed.

Their persecution was more subtle but no less real. Employers were told to fire family members. Landlords were warned not to rent to family members. Even less immediate family members and distant relatives were warned not to help. The results were near catastrophic. Families were not only deprived by having the primary breadwinner in jail but they also found themselves unable to get jobs and have places to live. Wives and daughters were often forced into prostitution. Few in Taiwan suffered more than the families of political prisoners.

In our weekly meetings with Peter, we talked about how we might help these families. Through our post office box in Hong Kong, we were able to exchange ideas with the Kagans, now back in Cambridge. We talked about the possibilities of supplying sewing machines and other equipment for cottage industries so the families could support themselves. Soon enough, we learned how naïve that idea was. The neediest of these families were in a survival mode without the luxury of setting up such businesses or even of carting the equipment from one place to another. The one way we could help them was with cash —if we could get it into the country.

In the fall of 1967, when the decision about my appointment to Taiwan Theological College had been made, I had been in full-time language study for a year and a half. I was to begin teaching at the seminary in January and attending language school part-time. Eventually, the seminary expected us to live in their housing on campus. The fact that none were currently available was a benefit. We rented a small house in Shih-lin, a suburb north of Taipei in the valley on the way to the seminary. The house, made of concrete blocks, was not more than 850 square feet and located at the end of a lane ending in a rice paddy. All of the houses were surrounded by six-foot walls. Across from the rice paddy was a bus stop where we could catch buses to Taipei or up the mountain to the seminary. We had the mimeograph machine tucked away in a closet and printed the first edition of the papers here.

Except that the residence of the Generalissimo and Mrs. Chiang Kai-shek lay on the other side of the rice paddy and main road, the location of our new home suited us fine. Our neighbors were all either Taiwanese or Mainlanders. There were no other foreigners in the neighborhood.

One of our first dinner guests in Shih-lin was J. Harry Haines, who had earlier been promised by the Methodist Board of Missions that he would teach church history at the seminary in Taipei. The promise was not fulfilled and the door opened to me when, in January 1966, Harry was appointed head of the Methodist Committee on Overseas Relief (MCOR). Harry was a native of New Zealand and former missionary in China and Malaysia. He had also been on the staff of the World Council of Churches in Geneva.

There weren't many places in the world where Harry had not been. He was a much sought-after speaker and quite a storyteller, especially about where he had been and what he had done. He had a smile that radiated compassion, and within a few years, it would make him one of the best-known Methodists in the world. After dinner, we sat on the only three padded chairs in our living room and talked. We listened with growing excitement as he told us what the MCOR was doing around the world. My ears perked up when he began talking about what they were doing in East Germany.

"We are not allowed into the country, but we have our ways of making a difference there," he said. "The fates of families of political prisoners in East Germany are deplorable. The state treats them as though they were guilty, too. There are probably no hungrier people anywhere in Europe than the families of political prisoners behind the Iron Curtain."

"What are you doing about it?" I said, hardly believing what I was hearing.

"We have found 'creative' ways to get money into the country and into the hands of these suffering people."

"Harry," I said, "we have found a similar problem here in Taiwan. There are hundreds, and perhaps thousands, of political prisoners here, and the government treats their families as if they were guilty, just like you describe in East

Germany. Do you think it would be possible for the MCOR to provide some funds to help these families?"

I could tell from the expression on his face frozen in a tight grimace that I had asked the wrong question.

"Of course not," was his unsmiling reply.

"Why?" I had the temerity to ask.

"It would be illegal."

"But, didn't you just tell me that the MCOR was smuggling money into East Germany?"

"They are godless communists!" he said with emphasis.

That ended the discussion and the evening.

"I've got to get back to the hotel," he said. "I've got an early flight to catch in the morning."

We walked in silence to the street at the end of our lane. He hailed a cab, gave instructions to the driver in passable Mandarin, and closed the door without saying good-bye.

I walked back to the house in shock, still not believing what I had heard. It was okay to take illegal actions to get MCOR money to the families of political prisoners in a communist country, but not in anticommunist Taiwan. My regret at raising the question quickly turned to concern about who he would now tell about our proposal.

It would have been easy for me to be cynical about church agencies after that night. But we had another visit from another denominational representative. A man who identified himself as DeWitt Barnett called the house one day. He said that a mutual friend suggested he get in touch with us when he came through Taiwan. We had many such calls, mostly from Methodists; this was the first from a Quaker. We arranged to meet him.

Tall with slightly stooped shoulders as if from a lifetime of getting down to the level of other people, he looked out at us from behind his beard and mustache. Looking like a shabby college professor in his worn tweed jacket, DeWitt quickly put us at ease by his open and easy manner.

"I'm the black sheep of my family," he said with an impish grin. "I'm the only Quaker in the family."

"What do you do?"

"Oh, do you have time to write down this title?" he asked with a laugh. "I'm supposed to say that I am the Quaker International Affairs Representative in East Asia for the American Friends Service Committee (AFSC). I promise I won't ever say it again. I am based in Japan."

DeWitt had been born to missionary parents in Shanghai in 1917. His father had been the head of the YMCA there. His brother, Doak, was a leading scholar and government advisor on China. China was in DeWitt's blood, but he came to us to talk about Taiwan. Not much conversation was necessary for us to decide to give him a set of the papers. He said he would read them carefully, and he did. In a couple of days, we scheduled a secret meeting with Peter.

We spent a long evening hearing Peter tell his story and offer his perspective on Taiwan again.

"I understand you were in Nagasaki when the atomic bomb was dropped there." he said. He knew about it because we had told him.

"I was actually on the outskirts of town. I was a student and recovering from the loss of my arm in a bombing raid." Peter patiently explained the loss of his arm and the devastation in Nagasaki.

"You were recently in prison, weren't you?" DeWitt asked, switching the subject back to Taiwan. "It must have been very difficult for you and your family."

"I was sentenced to eight years, as was Wei; Hsieh was sentenced to ten. In a magnanimous gesture on the centennial of Sun Yat-sen's death," Peter said with obvious sarcasm, "the Generalissimo ordered my release and reduced Wei and Hsieh's sentences by half. Wei will be released later this year."

"I receive the Amnesty International newsletter and understand that there are a lot of political prisoners here," DeWitt said.

"No one knows how many, not even the government," Peter said. "Those in prison are tortured and live in inhumane conditions, but many of their families suffer almost as much as they do."

"Isn't there something that could be done for the families?" DeWitt asked.

"We want to help them," Peter said, "but the government won't allow it, so if anything is done it will have to be done secretly and at great risk."

"I would like to help. I would like to make a contribution now," DeWitt said, pulling out his wallet.

"We don't have a way to help them yet," Peter said.

"If I could raise money in the U.S.," DeWitt said, "could you get it into the country and to the people who need it?"

"We can get it into the country, and we think we can get it to families who need it," Peter said.

The American Friends Service Committee was known for both its pacifism and its concern for human need. Still, DeWitt surprised us with his readiness to do something, something he knew to be illegal. I also wondered if the AFSC would be willing to give money on the terms we would have to have.

"The money would have to come into Taiwan in U.S. currency," I volunteered because we had already talked this through with Peter. "We will not be able to provide any kind of a paper trail for the use of the money. Records would be too dangerous to expect the courier to keep. The AFSC would only have our word that the money was actually getting to families."

"I think they will understand," DeWitt said. "I'm going back to Philadelphia in a couple of weeks, and I will see what I can do."

After he left that night, we tried to restrain the excitement we all felt. In the back of my mind was the worry that, whatever DeWitt's intentions, he might run into a bureaucratic brick wall in Philadelphia. But each of us felt there was something about the man that inspired confidence.

Within a few weeks, word came from DeWitt through Hong Kong that the project had been approved and they were beginning to raise money for it. How and where should funds be sent?

Chapter Twelve
Idealist to Realist

An idealist believes the short run doesn't count.
A cynic believes the long run doesn't matter.
A realist believes that what is done or left undone
in the short run determines the long run.

— Sydney J. Harris (1917-1986)

Had the American Friends Service Committee heard some of the discussions I had with Peter, they might have questioned my commitment to nonviolence. Two years earlier, when we told Peter that we would do things that might get us arrested or deported, Judith and I had said that we would not be party to anything that would result in violence. I regarded myself as a spiritual child of Martin Luther King Jr. and the Civil Rights movement wherein, as Dr. King often said, "the center of nonviolence is the principle of love." As much as I wanted to believe that, I could never completely embrace pacifism. I often confessed the inability as a failure rather than a principle of conscience.

My most important mentor in the seminary, albeit through the printed word, Reinhold Niebuhr, created that seed of doubt I could not shake, no matter how much I wanted to be true to Dr. King. Pointing to the reality of the coercion in nonviolence in how Gandhi's boycott of British cotton resulted in the undernourishment of children in England, Niebuhr argued that "once the factor of coercion is ethically justified... we cannot draw any absolute line of demarcation between violent and nonviolent coercion."[15] No matter the number of qualifications he put around it, and

---

[15] Reinhold Niebuhr, *Moral Man and Immoral Society: A Study in Ethics and Politics* (New York: Charles Scribner's Sons, 1932) p. 172.

he put a lot, ultimately the line between violent and nonviolent coercion was not absolute.

Each week, it seemed, brought new bad news about people being arrested or disappearing and new stories of torture from inside the prisons. What could end Chiang's charade of Taiwan as "Free China" and the justification of martial law by the claim that the civil war was not over? With Taiwan's growing importance to the U.S. war effort in Vietnam, the chances that the U.S. would be morally torn over supporting this dictator in Taiwan diminished.

As 1968 unfolded, we continued with our plan of nonviolent actions, giving packets to interested visitors and arranging meetings with Peter and other dissident Taiwanese. We worked on a plan to receive and distribute money to the families of political prisoners. The more detailed the plan got for getting money into the country and distributed on island, the more it was clear that to make the plan work, others (foreigners and Taiwanese) would be at considerable risk. It was one thing to have a post office box in Hong Kong and put letters with people going to and coming from Taiwan; it was yet another to involve them in smuggling money.

In the spring, a trip south to Ali Shan, an old Japanese resort high in the mountains in southern Taiwan, in the cherry blossom season sounded like the break we needed. The McKeels had suggested it. On April 2 Judith and the McKeels took the train south from Taipei. I taught my Monday classes in Tainan and headed north. We met in Chai-yi, where we boarded a small train on a narrow-gauge railroad built by the Japanese in 1912 for logging the area's giant cedars.

After several delightful days, on April 5 our party boarded the narrow-gauge railway for the trip back. We sat on hardwood benches for the six-hour trip down through three climate zones to reach Chia-yi.

Somewhere approximately halfway down, there were two sets of tracks where trains coming up could pass those coming down. When the two trains stopped, the morning newspapers available in Chia-yi were distributed on the train coming down. I could manage speaking Chinese but my reading skills were limited. The only papers on the train were in Chinese, so I didn't try to buy one. As people around me opened their papers to read, I saw that the front page consisted of one huge Chinese character I recognized as "wang," the character for "king." I wondered why the front page of a major newspaper would be covered with this character. Was there some important news about a king somewhere? My curiosity overcame my embarrassment at having to admit that I couldn't understand the headline.

"Please, sir," I said in Chinese to a man sitting in front of me beside his wife and two children, "I do not understand the headline. Did a king die?"

He turned around and looked at me.

"It is your country's Dr. King. He has been assassinated," the man said.

Then he opened the inside of the paper and pointed to two articles on page two.

"Can you read?" he asked politely.

I nodded my head. I could read the headlines well enough to know that there were race riots all over the United States. The second article was about an elementary school class somewhere that cheered when the teacher told them the news. The man shook his head as if he found the stories as hard for him to believe as they were for me to decipher.

I shared the news with Judith, Jane and Wayne. Jane and Wayne were both from Tennessee. We all wept.

At Chai-yi we boarded the tourist train for Taipei. There wasn't much talk. The exhilarating beauty of the cherry blossoms at Ali Shan faded as I was preoccupied with thoughts about Dr. King. I wondered if the death of King was also the beginning of the death of the movement to bring about change by nonviolent means. Before his death, the voices of Huey Newton and Bobby Seale through the Black Panther Party had pronounced King's nonviolent campaign dead and embraced violence as a means to get equality.

Newton and Seale weren't the only ones challenging the premise that nonviolence was moral and violence was immoral.

Peter and I had earlier talked about whether King's nonviolent approach would work in Taiwan.

"It will not work here," Peter said over and over. "You have to have some semblance of the rule of law for it to work. Even Gandhi had to have it in India. Here, they would just shoot us."

"Is violent revolution the only alternative?" I asked.

"When one side has all of the power, armed insurrection is simply suicide," he said, not as a principle but as a reality.

I had asked Peter if he had read Niebuhr, and he said he hadn't. I told him about how important *Moral Man and Immoral Society* had been for me. He said he would like to read it. He took my copy and within a couple of days he returned having not only read it but also having made three pages of typed notes to use in our conversation. He called attention to a footnote reference to Robert Briffault's *Rational Evolution:*

> No resistance to power is possible while the sanctioning lies, which justify that power, are accepted as valid. While that first and chief line of defense is unbroken there can be no revolt. Before any injustice, any abuse or oppression can be resisted, the lie upon which it is founded must be unmasked, must be clearly recognized for what it is. [16]

That is what Peter, Wei, and Hsieh had been trying to do in 1964, and it is what he was continuing now.

"There aren't any shortcuts to justice, are there?" I asked with some resignation apparent in my voice.

"We are doing the right things now," Peter said. "We are unmasking the lie on which this regime depends for its power."

"And the aid to the families?" I asked.

---

[16] Cited in Niebuhr, *Moral Man and Immoral Society*, p. 31.

"We must do that because they are suffering terribly and because we can help them," he said.

In Hong Kong, Bud agreed not only to receive and transmit mail to us, but he also agreed to do the same thing with money. He received the checks, cashed them, and exchanged them for U.S. currency in ten and twenty dollar bills. It was one thing to ask someone to carry letters; it seemed another to ask them to bring in illegal money. On several occasions Bud found reason to visit Taiwan and bring money. At no small risk to himself, he would put the bills in a money belt around his waist and not declare it when he came through customs. The problem was that we could not count on getting money with any regularity and we didn't have a way yet to get the money to the families.

Both of those problems were solved in the fall of 1968. Jim and Mary Ella Brentlinger, a missionary couple from Oregon, arrived in Taiwan in 1967 to begin language study. In the summer of 1968, Jim was assigned the job of field treasurer in both Taiwan and Hong Kong. For a while he went to Hong Kong for a week each month. At the end of 1968, they moved to Hong Kong, but Jim commuted back to Taiwan on the same schedule.

When his assignment was announced in the summer of 1968, I met Jim outside the Taipei railroad station where we were free to walk and talk. I asked him if he would be willing to carry some mail to and from Hong Kong. He immediately agreed but said the less he knew about what he would be carrying the better. From then on, each month Jim would take what mail we wanted to send out and bring mail back, some of it money in envelopes carefully packed and sealed by Bud. His regular trips meant that we were able to count on a continual supply of funds.

The second thing that happened to make our project feasible was that on September 20, after four years, Wei was released from prison. Peter arranged for us to meet him within a week of his release. He was one of our first visitors after moving into faculty housing on the seminary campus. When we met him, Peter had already talked to him about the family aid project, and he had volunteered to be the courier.

Round-faced with heavy black eyebrows over thick glasses, Wei was short and stocky, not fat but muscular. My impression the first time he came to our house was of a kind and gentle man, not what I expected from a thirty-three-year-old who had resisted his inquisitors at every point, even challenging the court and his guards to kill him. While in prison, Wei kept himself in peak physical condition, jogging every time he got into the prison yard and continuing exercises in whatever kind of cell he was in.

He was out of prison but was still followed by a couple of agents wherever he went. At least they tried. Wei treated it like a game. He would often take to the mountains for several hours of vigorous hiking or running, putting the physical stamina of his surveillance squad to the ultimate test. With his own joyful perversity, he was known to begin these jaunts on the last hour of his followers' shift, delaying their return to headquarters by hours.

On that first visit, Wei greeted us and then spoke to our two-and-a-half-year-old daughter standing across the room behind a chair.

"Is your name Li-hwa?" he asked in Chinese.

She nodded. Before long, Wei was sitting on the floor talking with her in Mandarin. He might have snuck in a little of his native Hakka, but if he did neither he nor Elizabeth said so. Not many weeks after that, he would be assisting me in translating my history lectures into Chinese.

Before he left that first day, he told us that he was ready to take money to some families who were in desperate need of aid. He and Hsieh had gathered as much information about the location and situation of families as they could from the prisoners.

After the first distribution, he brought back a written record of those to whom he had given money. We talked about it and agreed that records should not be made. Wei had discovered what we feared. Many of the families had moved on from where the loved ones in prison thought they were. And their situations were usually worse than the prisoners knew. He found only half of the families he sought, and a couple of them were too frightened to take money from him. The others, he said, expressed their gratitude. I found it hard to believe that Wei was willing to take the great risks involved in the distribution, knowing that if he were caught he would go back to prison and perhaps never come out. That never seemed to be a consideration to Wei.

In my head, the question about the morality or immorality of the use of violence was still not resolved. Peter had rightly pointed out that we had important work to do that didn't require an answer to the question. Because one man listened and brave people were willing to take risks, that important work could now go forward.

Chapter Thirteen
An Impossible Project Born

If one is forever cautious,
can one remain a human being?

—Aleksandr Solzhenitsyn (1918-2008)

After the trip to Ali Shan and the assassination of Dr. King, I was content doing, as Peter called it, "the work we can do"—the occasional distribution of packets, arranging meetings of visitors with Peter, and making the final arrangements for the distribution of aid to families. Part of the work I could do was to teach at the seminary, and I was discovering how I loved to teach. Each day in class seemed to validate my sense of the call to be a teacher. For the most part, my students and the non-missionary faculty were Taiwanese.

The fact that I was teaching in Mandarin rather than Taiwanese—the language used in most classes, worship, faculty meetings, and student gatherings—was a bit of an anomaly. Chiang's government had declared Mandarin to be the official language of the island; it was the required language of educational institutions. The Presbyterian church was engaged in a running battle with the government on its insistence on using Taiwanese. There were periodic raids by security officers at churches and the denominational headquarters to confiscate and destroy church material in Taiwanese. The PCT refused to acquiesce. It was a continuing struggle and was not just about pride, I sensed, but also about identity. The students seemed to give me a pass because they knew I was Methodist, and Methodist missionaries were required to learn Mandarin; they were less forgiving toward a couple of older Presbyterian missionaries who had earlier experience on the Mainland and didn't speak Taiwanese.

The first class I taught at the seminary was New Testament Greek. The regular teacher left to study abroad, and I was assigned to teach the class. After all, on my resume there was that year of teaching Greek at SMU six years earlier. When I thought about it, the prospect was almost laughable. I was teaching Greek in Mandarin to native-speaking Taiwanese using an English text.

In the summer of 1968 I was not only preparing to teach a full load in the fall—ecumenics, history of Western civilization, and the history of Christianity in the nineteenth and twentieth centuries—but I was also sent as a delegate by the seminary to a month-long meeting in Hong Kong with church history teachers from seventeen other seminaries throughout Southeast Asia. We enjoyed a seminar with the dean of mission historians from the University of Chicago, R. Pierce Beaver, but our main purpose was to organize a professional society of church history and begin the organizational work for a Southeast Asia graduate school of theology with courses to be offered in Taiwan, Hong Kong, the Philippines, Singapore, and Malaysia.

The month was a heady experience that made me even more excited about teaching. When I got back to Taiwan, some sober realities diminished the exhilaration. Judith had suffered a miscarriage and had been taken by the McKeels to their home to recuperate. And now they were leaving for Wayne's new assignment in Bolivia. Our house was ready at the seminary, and the principal was anxious for us to get moved in. We needed to make the move before the semester started in mid-September.

One night in early September of 1968, Gene Ethridge was at our house in Shih-lin for dinner with Peter. Had they not been good friends and regulars at the house, we wouldn't have been entertaining guests. The house was in chaos with boxes everywhere as we prepared for the move up the mountain. But these two were more like family than guests. Gene was a missionary of the Presbyterian Church U.S. from Georgia who was assigned to work with university students. His irreverence toward most things "missionary" and the propaganda of the KMT drew us together. What he lacked in Taiwanese—he was assigned a short term and worked in English—he made up for by his identification with the students. He was open, and they trusted him. Soon after we became friends, he began distributing packets and helping plan the family aid project.

"I had dinner out two nights ago," Peter said as we ate. "I was entertained by an official from the Investigative Bureau at a special house they have for such affairs."

"What happened?" I asked.

"After the dinner, the one in charge smiled and said, 'You know, you could have an accident any time and be killed.'" Peter paused and then went on, "I think they are planning to kill me. I have a friend with connections in the Investigative Bureau who says that they actually have a plan for me to have an 'accident.'"

We didn't speak and waited for Peter to go on. Peter had told us of other encounters and veiled threats, but this time he seemed to take it more seriously. He tried to lighten the mood by changing the subject, but the rest of us were stuck on the threat.

Gene had an evening English class on the other side of Taipei, so at half past seven he excused himself, mounted his Vespa motor scooter, and headed down the lane. Not five minutes later there was an urgent knock at the gate. Gene pushed his scooter inside the gate, looked back down the lane, and then he motioned me to lock the gate. He said nothing as he pushed me back inside the house.

In the light I could see that his face had gone pale.

"When I got to the end of the lane," he said, almost gasping for breath, "there were seven or eight gray suits [secret police]. I turned right to go up to the main road, and there were eight or ten more."

"Did they stop you?" I asked, feeling a little breathless myself.

"No, I didn't have my helmet on because I was about to light a cig. I think they saw that I was a foreigner and didn't stop me. They must be here for Peter!" he blurted out.

"No one followed me here. I'm sure of that," Peter said with less confidence than usual.

"There's no other reason why all of them would be down there. It's the only way in here and the only way out," Gene said.

"What do we do?" I asked the others. "Maybe they followed him to the area but lost him before he came down the lane," I continued without waiting for an answer. "If that's the case, they will simply go house to house until they get to us."

"I will leave," Peter said. "If they don't know which house I'm in, maybe you won't be arrested, too. If they knew of your relationship to me, they would have already been here."

Peter reached for his coat, but Gene stopped him.

"Our only chance is for you to ride out on the scooter with me," Gene said. "They didn't stop me before. Maybe if you wear the helmet and your raincoat, they won't stop us."

"I can't allow you to take that kind of chance," Peter said.

"It's not up to you this time, Peter," Gene said looking to Judith and me for confirmation.

"He's right," I said. "It's our one chance and we've got to take it."

I picked up Peter's raincoat, which he hadn't worn because it wasn't raining, and helped him put it on. We said good-bye not knowing when or if we would see either of them again.

"If I don't call you within an hour," Gene said, "you'll know that we didn't get through, and then you can...hell! I don't know what you do then. Whatever it is, do it."

Before opening the gate, Peter put on the large plastic helmet with the visor down. Gene cranked the scooter and the engine made its putt-putt start. Peter threw his leg over the back and sat behind Gene, who took Peter's arms and pulled them around his waist. As soon as they were through the gate, I closed and locked it, not daring to peek to see what would happen at the other end of the lane.

That would have been a foolish risk. If they were stopped, there was nothing we could do.

Although the night was cool, I was drenched in a nervous sweat waiting for another knock at the gate. In low voices, we talked about what we would do if they didn't get through and they didn't find us. We would call the U.S. Embassy, we said, to file a report about Gene. We would find a way to get word to Mrs. Peng. If Fox was still in Taipei, we would call him. But we knew if they were stopped, there would be no fix for Peter.

We talked for what seemed like hours, but twenty minutes after they left, the phone rang.

"It's okay!" Gene said when he recognized my voice answering the phone. "We're fine. I'll talk to you tomorrow." And he hung up.

I don't think either Judith or I had ever been as emotionally spent, not even after that night at Peter's house. I couldn't even imagine what Peter and Gene went through.

"We've got to get him out of the country!" one of us said, but it was what both of us were thinking. We weren't the only ones.

"I don't know why they didn't stop us," Gene said the next day when we met in town. "We passed within five feet of several of them. They just looked at us through those damn dark glasses that some of 'em wear at night—the dumbasses. I waved at them while I was trying to keep from peeing in my pants."

"Are you sure you weren't followed?" I asked.

"I don't think so, but I guess you can't be sure."

"What about Peter?" I asked.

"He had me drop him off in front of a large hotel on Chung Shan North Road where there were a lot of people going in and out. He said he would take a taxi from there. I didn't think he was going to stop shaking my hand thanking me."

"We've got to get him out of Taiwan!" Gene said with almost the same words Judith and I had used the night before. "I don't know how we can do it, but we've got to find a way."

A couple of days later, I was chatting with a Mainlander neighbor whose kids often played in the lane with Elizabeth.

"There were a lot of men in gray suits around here a couple of nights ago," I said, fishing for information.

"Oh," he said, laughing, "they were special security people charged with guarding the president. There have been some burglaries in the area and since we are so close to his residence it was a major security concern. They caught the burglars."

That knowledge did nothing to diminish the determination we made that night to get Peter out. It occurred to me how the woman who accused us of hubris on the papers project would fall down laughing at the thought that a couple of missionaries with no relevant experience might attempt to engineer the escape of one of Chiang's chief threats from this locked-down state. I didn't have time to think about our audacity; convincing Peter he had to leave was the first problem.

Chapter Fourteen
Making It Happen

Start by doing what's necessary;
then do what's possible;
and suddenly you are doing the impossible.

— St. Francis of Assisi (1182-1226)

The next time we met, I told Peter about our conversation with Gene and how we were in agreement that he needed to leave Taiwan. We recalled how he had received invitations from both the University of Michigan and McGill University to come and teach in their institutions, only to have the authorities warn him not even to apply for an exit permit. To do so "would only embarrass our government," they told him. We knew they would not let him leave legally.

During the fall of 1968 we often discussed the possibility of his escaping the island. Sometimes he would say that he wasn't willing to leave Taiwan. He had a responsibility to his country and he couldn't bear the thought of leaving his family behind. At other times he would allow us to make the case for why he should leave—pent-up as he was, he couldn't exercise leadership and, most important, they were likely to kill him, in which event he would be no good to his country or his family. Although we had known Peter now for more than two years and saw each other almost weekly, I suspected that he harbored doubts that these well-meaning friends of his were capable of such a feat. If he did, he was not alone. Sometimes I would wake up at night and wonder what kind of fantasy I was having to think we might actually create a plan that could be successful. The awful reality, I would remind myself, was that if we didn't get him out, he was going to be murdered.

The prospect of his assassination did not stop me from thinking about the long-term consequences if we were successful in getting him out. Outside, he would no doubt provide leadership for Taiwanese abroad who wanted independence, those who were a part of the different organizations advocating it and those who weren't. But for how long could he be away from Taiwan and still expect to return as the leader he was when he left? Five years? The longer he was out of the country, the more remote the chances that he could lead the Taiwanese people would become. And then I would ask who the hell I thought I was asking these questions. I didn't have a clue about the answers. Besides, for me and the others involved, the real possibility of his being murdered trumped all of those speculations.

We didn't talk about escape every time Peter came to the house. It was too heavy, especially when we didn't have any good answers. But at every opportunity, I talked with foreign friends I could trust. In January 1969, Mark and Jenny Thelin came up with their toddler Karl to stay overnight with us at the seminary. Mark was a professor of sociology at Tunghai University in Taichung and had been there for many years. He had met Peter through George Todd in 1963. When Peter was arrested in 1964, Mark visited the Peng family whenever he came to Taipei.

The purpose of our meeting was to brainstorm ways that Peter might leave Taiwan unnoticed. Since Peter did not arrive at the house until after midnight, the conversation took most of the rest of the night. We walked through what seemed like endless scenarios in which he would leave on a fishing boat from Kaohsiung or Taichung or on a freighter from Keelung. The problem with these possibilities was that neither Peter nor we had any reliable personal connections with the people who owned boats or were in positions to get him onto a ship. We had no doubt that there were people who could be bribed, but the search for those individuals seemed to expose the plan to unacceptable risks. Because of the level of security at the airports, we didn't consider the possibility of his escaping by plane.

Going out by boat seemed to be the only possibility. And if it was, then we had to find a way to make it work. We agreed to work on it. Mostly, that meant Peter had to try to think of any contacts he had with whom he dared to broach the subject. An hour or so before daylight, when we ended the evening, we congratulated ourselves on clarifying the possibilities. I wondered if we had not succeeded in convincing Peter of the futility of any attempt.

Within days of the meeting with Mark, Judith or I read a story in a news magazine about how a man escaped from East to West Germany. This is the way it worked: A person from West Germany crossed legally into East Germany for a visit. While there he gave his passport to the person wanting to escape. The East German used the passport with his own picture inserted to go through the checkpoint to the West. That was on a Friday night. The West German then went to his embassy in East Berlin on Monday morning when the offices were opened after the weekend and reported his passport lost or stolen. He was given a replacement and returned safely to West Germany.

For the first time since we started talking about the escape, I felt an excitement that this might actually work with Peter. When we next met, I thought I sensed a glimmer of excitement in Peter, too.

Together, the three of us discussed what would be required to make this work.

"The first and biggest question is who we can get to come into Taiwan and take this risk with their passport," I said.

"It has to be a nationality that you can pass for, Peter," Judith said.

"It would have to be a foreigner, not someone with a Taiwan passport," Peter said. "Some Taiwanese independence activists in Japan might be willing to help. I can ask them."

"The second thing we will need," I said, "is money."

"Once we hear back from Japan and decide if this is what we're going to do," Judith said, "we can contact our friends who are now back in the U.S.—George Todd, Don

Wilson, Dick and Leigh Kagan, Gene Ethridge, and Sid and Judy Hormell. I believe they can get the money."

"The third thing is a place for Peter to go," I said.

"I can't go to the United States," Peter said, "at least not right away. I don't think they would guarantee me political asylum because it would upset their KMT friends too much," he said, laughing. "Since I have been corresponding with people at Amnesty International in Sweden for several years, I can see if they can arrange asylum for me."

Over the next months, Peter corresponded with Japan and Sweden. We corresponded with our friends in the U.S. Since we had to send mail out by way of Hong Kong and receive responses once a month from there, the slow pace was maddening. Peter didn't have to wait too long for a positive response from Japan. They would find a Japanese national who, in exchange for a ticket and a few hundred dollars for a weekend in Taipei, would come and "lose" his passport. In May, Peter received a letter from Sweden saying that they were sure he would be welcome there. In July he received another letter confirming that he would be granted political asylum if he made it as far as Stockholm.

Before he completed his term and left Taiwan in the summer of 1969, Gene Ethridge promised that he would see that the money for the escape was raised. On October 3, I received a letter from Gene through Bud in Hong Kong saying that he had attended a meeting in New York that included the Kagans, the Youngs, Don Wilson, Feli Carrino, and the Hormells. Gene said he was not sure enough of the security of the mail system to write about what they had decided to do. He said they would get the job done.

We could hardly believe how things were falling into place. With each new letter from outside, the plan became more real, and as it became more real, more decisions were required. In the summer of 1969, we set the target for getting Peter out of the country at the end of the year. We wanted to do it earlier, but with the time communication required with Hong Kong, Japan, and the U.S., we realized that we would be lucky to be ready by then.

The people in Japan would arrange for who would be involved there and who would know the operational details. Who, besides Judith and I, would be involved in Taiwan? Bud was a part of each stage of the planning from Hong Kong. By this time, Jim and Mary Ella Brentlinger had moved to Hong Kong, but Jim was commuting to Taiwan monthly just as he had to Hong Kong before. He knew nothing of the plan, but his regular trips in and out of the country were critical to its success. The McKeels had gone to their new posting in Bolivia. Gene Ethridge had completed his term with the Presbyterians and returned to Georgia. Jamie and Carol Long, assigned to teach at Soochow for two years and who had participated in some of the early planning for the escape, were finishing their term in August of 1969.

When the Longs left in August, they carried with them a critical letter from Peter to the people in Japan. They were to find the person in Tokyo and hand deliver it. They couldn't find the person able to make contact, so they waited until they got to the U.S. and then mailed it back to Japan.

We decided that we would not involve any Taiwanese in the plan; to do so was a death sentence for them if the plan failed. We continued to work with Wei and then with Hsieh when he got out of prison in September of 1969 to distribute money to families of political prisoners, but we would not involve them in this. We didn't have any doubts about their competence or dependability; it was our competence and dependability I worried about. Peter had to take the risk with us, but neither Wei nor Hsieh did. At least that was what made sense to us.

We needed some other colleagues in Taipei that could help us finish the plan and then implement it. Mark Thelin in Taichung and Rowland Van Es in Tainan were too far away. We needed some foreigners the authorities would have no reason to suspect. And we found them. George and Dot Hoover were United Methodist missionaries appointed for work in Singapore doing Chinese language study in Taiwan. They had gone through the Missionary Orientation Center training at Stony Point. Taller than my six–foot-four-inch frame, George towered over most people, especially in Taiwan. He was a community organizer in the Saul Alinsky tradition and politically savvy. Dot was a nurse and, as far as I was ever able to see, feared nobody. After they met Peter and we talked to them about being involved in the escape, they didn't hesitate for a moment.

Another couple arrived in Taiwan who had gotten to know the Hoovers at Stony Point. Mike and Judy Heath were on their way to Sarawak as agricultural missionaries, stopping in Taiwan for a year's language study. They were both from ranch families in Wyoming. Tall and slender, Mike looked every bit the cowboy he was. Judy was red-headed and as even-tempered as Mike. Once they met Peter, they too said they would do whatever they could.

In addition to the important new perspectives and questions they brought to the plan, their apartments in Taipei gave us new places to have our regular meetings with Peter. In the fall of 1969, there was no indication that Judith or I had gotten the attention of any of the security agencies, but we wanted to take no unnecessary chances.

The Hoovers and Heaths also lightened Judith's and my workload. In the fall, both of us were teaching full loads at the seminary, and being named registrar had given me new responsibilities. I had also been assigned to a team to develop a plan to unite the two seminaries. The PCT was under pressure from the government to withdraw from the World Council of Churches because it advocated the recognition of the People's Republic. The United Methodist Mission Board had finally lost its patience with its "chaplaincy to Mainlanders" and convened a consultation with the Methodist Church in Taiwan with a view to withdrawing its financial support. In addition to being our busiest fall for "missionary work" since our arrival, a new member was about to join our family.

Given all that was going on in our lives that fall in 1969, we had not planned on an addition to our family. After the birth of Elizabeth, we had applied for the adoption of a child from the Christian Children's Home in Taiwan. Judith and I had always wanted to adopt, even before we knew that Judith's giving birth to another child would be dangerous. It didn't matter if the child was Chinese, Taiwanese, Anglo, or any other race, although given where we lived and the agency to which we had applied, it was most likely that the baby would be Chinese or Taiwanese.

On Friday, October 17, we received a call from Mrs. Graber at the home in Taichung. She said that she had a baby and wanted us to come down to talk about it. There was, she said, an Eurasian boy (born on Thursday) that we could have if all of the legalities are taken care of—which in this case, she assured us, should be no problem. Since he was premature, however, it would be a few days before we could have him.

The call could not have come at a more inopportune time, but we didn't hesitate. If a baby was available, we wanted it.

The "few days" became ten. On Monday, October 27, Sue Fowler, a volunteer representative for the home, took the baby from the hospital in Taipei to her home, where she waited for the woman to come who would take him down to Taichung to be registered. At her house, we saw the beautiful baby that was to be Richard Lancaster Thornberry. She had to take him down to Taichung to the orphanage so that he could be registered there as "left on the doorstep," a convenient euphemism to allow birthmothers not be named should that be their choice. And that was Richard's mother's choice. On Wednesday we took the train down and picked up our new son. He was so small that we carried him back on the train swaddled in a blanket in a woven peach basket.

Within two weeks, Richard was losing all of his food through projectile vomiting and losing weight. It took another week to confirm a diagnosis of pyloric stenosis, a congenital condition where muscles in the stomach become enlarged to the point of preventing food from entering the small intestine. Immediate surgery was called for, but because Richard was already so weak, he had to gain some strength. We were referred to an American surgeon, Ben Dykstra. Dykstra, a Reformed Church missionary at the Presbyterian McKay Hospital in Taipei, had studied this very surgery on his last furlough.

Dykstra operated on Richard November 18, and he came through fine. He was back in the incubator, where he had spent the first ten days of his life outside the womb, for another ten days. Not being able to hold our little baby, who was not a lot heavier now than at his birth, was an emotional drain even though we recognized that the surgeon had saved his life.

Richard came home and began gaining weight. Some kind of equilibrium returned to our lives, and along with it deep gratitude to the Hoovers and Heaths for meeting regularly with Peter and keeping the preparations for the escape going.

We wanted to give Richard a Chinese name that included part of Peter's name. Even though Peter rarely visited our house once we were in the last months of the escape plan, he insisted on coming to see Richard.

"We want you to name him and for him to have a part of your name," I said, holding the baby up for Peter's inspection.

"He will, of course, have 'T'ang' for Thornberry," he said. "The first character of his given name should be *Chih* [pronounced *jr*], meaning 'a strong will to achieve for a higher purpose.' Then, we can give him *Ming* from my name, which means 'bright' or 'clear.'"

"What would the combination of *Chih* and *Ming* mean?" I asked.

"It would mean someone who can guide others with clarity and understanding," he said.

"That's wonderful!" Judith exclaimed.

We thanked him profusely and let him get on down the mountain, feeling some guilt that we had violated the protocol we had established by having him visit us at the seminary in the last phase of preparations.

When there was a knock at the door a half an hour later, the last person we expected to see was Peter.

"I got down to Shih-lin," Peter said, sounding out of breath, "and remembered that we can't have your baby named Chih-Ming. That's the Chinese *mingdze* for Ho Chi-min, the president of North Vietnam. It would not be good to give the same name to a baby in Taiwan."

"What are we going to do?" Judith asked.

"I think we should name him T'ang Chih-Min, using the second character of my given name, which means 'intelligent' or 'alert,'" Peter said. "It means he will be a wise leader. That name will be much better for him in this country."

As quickly as Peter had come, he left, as if to mitigate the risk he had run by coming not once but twice to the house.

Chapter Fifteen
Countdown

Fear is an emotion indispensable for survival.

— Hannah Arendt (1906-1975)

Even though Judith and I were distracted, we attended the weekly planning meetings with Peter, the Hovers, and the Heaths. Peter was to go out disguised as a Japanese hippie musician, and we would put a picture of him in that disguise in the "lost" passport. During the fall of 1969, he conducted an experiment. For four weeks, he grew a beard with a mustache but did not go out of his house during the day. He still came out after midnight and met with us at either the Hoovers or the Heaths. During this time he didn't show himself to his watchers. When the beard was as he wanted it, he cut it off, satisfied that in the four weeks immediately before his departure he would grow it again.

Before he cut off his beard, Peter went to a do-it-yourself passport photo booth and took a number of pictures. The pictures were sent to Munakata Takayuki in Japan. He had found Abe Kenichi, a Japanese national who was willing to come to Taiwan and "lose" his passport. Munakata acquired an embosser made like that used by the Japanese government on passports. With the passport of the man coming in hand, they embossed ten or twelve of the pictures so that one of them would match the picture we would put in place of the original perfectly. Then, they sent the pictures back to us in Taiwan.

We had all agreed on the disguise and thought Peter looked like the Japanese hippie musician he would pretend to be. What would we do about his arm?

"How can we keep his arm from being a dead give away?" Mike asked with the simple honesty that we had come to expect of him. We had talked about the question before but not in such blunt terms and not in Peter's presence.

"I'll tell you what I can do," Dot said. "Instead of hoping that they won't notice his arm, I'll wrap it like I've done it for serious burns many times in the hospital. They will notice it but what they will see is his arm in a sling with a large bandage from his elbow down. They won't think about his not having an arm."

"Yeah," I said, "he can even have a story about getting hot soup spilled on him at a restaurant in Taipei."

"Maybe I'll still be angry and considering suing the restaurant when I get back to Japan," Peter laughed, getting into the spirit of what almost seemed like a joke.

"I think the bandage will work," Judith said.

Peter agreed, and Dot said she would be prepared with the necessary supplies and equipment on the night of departure.

The date set was for Saturday, January 3, 1970. We were uncomfortable with a Saturday night departure. We thought that the best time was when a lot of people would be in the airport, but Peter wanted to leave at a time where there were the fewest people there. Outside his presence, we talked with the Hoovers and Heaths about the concern we all shared. We concluded that his peace of mind was probably more important in determining when he should make the attempt. So, Saturday night was the time.

There was another item related to Peter's peace of mind.

"Some of you will be at the airport to see that Peter gets onto the plane," said Judith, knowing only that it wouldn't be either of us; for security, it would be one of the new couples. "And Bud will be at the airport in Hong Kong. I wish we could have someone on the plane with Peter who can witness whatever happens there."

"That's a good idea," Peter said. "I would feel better if someone were there, but who do you think would do that?"

"It should not be anyone associated with the people you are dealing with in Japan," I said. Everybody nodded in agreement.

"What about DeWitt Barnett?" I said as the idea popped into my head.

"I don't know if he can do it," said Peter, "but we can ask him."

Within days the word was out. In an unrelated but timely visit by DeWitt to Taiwan on December 12 and 13, we had an opportunity to discuss it with him in person.

"Of course, I will do it," he said as if it weren't a question. "Tell me when and on what flight."

"Peter will go out on Saturday night, January 3," I said. "We want you to come in on the JAL flight from Japan and then be on board when Peter gets on in Taipei."

"Why don't I take that flight on Friday night so I can get here and meet with you and know that everything is as planned?" he asked.

I was about to say that I thought meeting Peter in person was an unwarranted risk, but Peter responded before I could speak.

"I think it is a good idea," Peter said. "I would like to see you before I go to the airport."

That settled that. Hopefully, when the flight left Taipei, Peter and DeWitt would be on it. If both were, we would have a witness to whatever might happen there.

In one of the few references to the escape that I recorded in my journal, on December 20 I wrote about word from Bud in Hong Kong: "Word came yesterday. The money is here. We are ready for the last stage." While we continued to have funds come in from the American Friends Service Committee for aid for families of political prisoners, there was never a question about using any of that money for the escape. All of that money went to the families. Our friends in the U.S. fulfilled their promise. I don't know if it is true or not, but I heard that Don was able to tap a Presbyterian "church beautification" fund for some of the money. With money in hand, we purchased a ticket for Saturday night, January 3, in the name of Abe, who was coming from Japan on Friday.

On Saturday night, we sent George and Dot to the airport to observe the departure of the 10:00 P.M. flight on which Peter would depart a week later. We waited for them at the Heaths' apartment. When they got back around eleven o'clock, both of their faces showed that the news was not good.

"There was absolutely no one in the airport," George said. He was as close to losing his cool as any time I had seen him.

"We went upstairs to the visitors' observation area that overlooks the whole departure area as well as the tarmac outside," Dot explained. "Once Peter enters the airport, except for when he leaves the departure area and goes through customs, we will be able to keep him in view until he boards the plane. What we saw tonight was disturbing," she said in her matter-of-fact way. "This was the last flight of the night. Even the other airline desks were closed, and there was only one clerk for our flight. No one! No one boarded the flight here."

"All we could see were security people wandering around," George said. "I think it is suicidal for you to attempt it on Saturday night, Peter. I think we need to reschedule your departure for midday Saturday or maybe for early the next week."

I could see the wheels turning in Peter's head. There was dead silence, and then he spoke.

"No," he said. "Let's not change the plan or the ticket; I think this is still the best time to try it."

Nothing more was said, but the Hoovers' report sobered us all, including Peter.

After Peter left that night, we stayed to talk with the others. There was no talk of trying to get Peter to change his mind. The decision had been made. But we moved on to a question that we had all thought about but hadn't discussed as a group.

"What do we do if Peter is arrested at the airport?" I asked.

"The only thing we will be able to do is to get word to our friends outside to publicize his arrest," George said in his matter-of-fact manner, now recovered from the experience at the airport.

"And, hopefully," I said, "we will be able to do that before we are arrested."

"Look," Judy said, breaking her usual silence at these gatherings, "we can't afford to have these hung-dog looks around Peter. We can't do it to ourselves either. We've got a plan and it's going to work!"

On Friday afternoon, January 2, Peter met Abe somewhere in town and brought his passport to the Heaths' apartment. It was time for one of the most critical operations of the plan: removing the Japanese man's picture from his passport and by replacing it with Peter's embossed photo. The embossed markings were in a circle— about a third of the circle on the bottom left-hand corner of the photograph, the rest on the page. From the article we had read about the escape from East Germany, I had learned that the photo needed to be split so that the base of the original would remain intact. The glue used by the passport agency was such that any attempt to remove the whole picture would result in tearing the paper underneath.

My task was to split the photo and paste it over the base of the original photo so that the new picture would have the same thickness as the original. In the weeks before, I had practiced using a thin razor blade on other pictures. I had done it enough to see that it could be done.

On Friday night, I split several of the pictures whose embossing looked like they would match the existing indentions best. We spent a long time deciding on the perfect match. Peter watched some of what was happening on the table but spent most of the time making small talk with those who weren't kibitzing at the table. After what must have seemed an eternity to Peter, the selection was made and we were ready for the application. Judith took glue, applied it to the base, and then carefully set it in place. The embossing matched perfectly.

Peter spent the last twenty-four hours at the Heaths' apartment. We and the Hoovers went home to sleep but were with Peter most of the rest of the time.

Late Friday night, probably early Saturday morning, Peter made one trip back to his home. He had not told his wife or his teenage son and daughter that he was leaving—

that knowledge would have made them culpable. He spoke of going into his children and wife's rooms while they slept and saying his silent good-byes. When he returned to the Heaths' apartment and told us, he cried. I think it was the only time I ever saw Peter cry. We cried with him.

By Saturday morning, everything had been done that could be done. With time on our hands, we played Oh Hell, an easy-to-learn trick-taking card game that Judith had learned years before. Unlike bridge, the object is to take exactly the number of tricks bid. Through the day we had a continuous game going on the dining room table with four of the seven of us rotating in and out.

When we gathered around the table for our last dinner together, we presented Peter with a cardigan sweater purchased by Judith and Dot as a sentimental going-away present.

"You are going to need this in Sweden," Judith said, handing him the unwrapped sweater.

"Thank you," Peter managed to get out. "Thank you all for what you've done."

Peter got up from his place at the table and walked over to his bag. For the second time in twenty-four hours, there were no dry eyes in the room.

DeWitt arrived on the flight from Japan Friday night. Peter wanted to go to the airport with him. We didn't think it was wise, but it seemed important to Peter. The Heaths' apartment was only about fifteen minutes from the airport. DeWitt arrived at about nine o'clock. While the rest of us greeted DeWitt and said our last good-byes to Peter, Dot and George left to get a cab so that they would be at the airport when Peter and DeWitt arrived.

When Peter and DeWitt arrived at the airport, they separated. The Hoovers had gone directly to the visitors' observation area. Apprehensive about their experience at the empty airport a week before, they were shocked and relieved to see a large group of Japanese tourists get off a bus and get in line to check in for the last flight of the night. Immediately behind them, Peter came in with his wig, beard, and bandaged arm carrying a guitar case. He was a Japanese musician in Taipei to play for the New

Year's festivities and had burned his arm. Peng fell into line with them and went through customs and out to the plane.

The Hoovers were ecstatic about their good fortune with the group of tourists. When Peter went into the customs area where they couldn't see him, they moved over to where they could see him emerge and walk out to where the plane was waiting. Just as Peter was about to ascend the steps of the plane, an official ran out of the terminal and led him back inside. George and Dot could see Peter looking up at them and thought it was over. Frozen in shock, they couldn't move.

Before they could leave, they saw Peter emerge by himself and head back to the airplane. The Hoovers didn't know why he had been taken back or why he was now boarding the plane. We later learned that in his nervousness Peter had left some of his documents on the custom official's counter. The official had come to get Peter to identify and collect his documents.

Hearts pounding, they watched the plane taxi all the way to the end of the runway. Then, it turned and taxied back to the terminal. For the second time, the Hoovers concluded that Peter had been discovered. Officials and airport personnel went in and out of the plane, but Peter didn't come out.

At the Heaths' apartment, we also believed that something had gone wrong. In the weeks before, Mike Heath had determined that this last flight of the night went almost directly over their apartment. Almost forty-five minutes after the normal departure time, there had been no takeoff.

"It hasn't been more than five minutes late since I've started checking," Mike said.

"Do you think we could have missed the sound of it taking off?" Judith asked.

"If you hear it," Mike said, "you'll know we didn't miss it."

No one said it, but all of us were thinking the worst.

The plane remained at the terminal for twenty minutes or so. Finally, those who had boarded the plane exited. No passengers got off. The plane's doors were closed and it taxied to the end of the runway. This time it took off.

"You're right about the sound, Mike," I said, raising my voice to be heard as the plane took off.

"We don't know what the delay means," Judith said.

And we fell into a nervous silence.

When the Hoovers finally arrived, they were so drained of emotion they could hardly speak. Then, the whole story tumbled out. Judy got out glasses and a bottle of wine; we had a toast.

After the celebration, we had one more task before going back home at the seminary. Before he left, Peter had given us a nine-by-thirteen-inch manila envelope and asked us to deliver it to his brother's house after the escape.

With few street lights, the streets were dark; the walls shielded most of whatever light might have come from the houses. Since it wasn't far, we walked. It was after midnight when we found the gate and rang the bell.

"Peng Ming-min asked us to give this to you," Judith said as she stepped into the small area of light that appeared with the opening of the gate and handed the envelope to Peter's sister-in-law.

In the shadows behind Judith, I don't think the sister-in-law was aware of my presence.

"Thank you! Thank you!" she said, taking the envelope without hesitation.

"It is very late," Judith said. "We apologize and won't disturb you longer."

"That doesn't matter," the sister-in-law said politely, dismissing the apology. "Thank you!" she said again as she closed the gate.

"Strange, it was almost as if she was expecting our visit," Judith mused as we made our way down the dark lane to a street where we could catch a cab,

It was well after midnight when we got back to our house at the seminary and began waiting for a call from Hong Kong.

When no call came by two o'clock that morning, I began to wonder if something had happened. I slept for a couple of hours but awoke even more anxious that the phone hadn't rung. We had agreed beforehand that we would not call Hong Kong but wait until Bud called us.

We didn't go to church. George called hoping to hear that we had news. When I said we hadn't, he suggested that he and Mike come up and shoot some baskets as something—anything!—to do while we waited. Judith stayed at the house by the phone. We were on the court when Judith came to give us the good news. In our own coded language, around "the birth of twins", Bud reported that Peter and DeWitt had arrived in Hong Kong safely, that they had stayed up all night talking, and that at midmorning Bud had put Peter on a plane bound for Sweden.

We continued shooting hoops—running, grunting, jumping, and yelling— and began to release the nervous tension that had been building up for months.

On Monday we received another call from Bud saying that Peter had sent a telegram from Copenhagen with the message that he was changing planes for the last leg of his journey and would soon be in Stockholm.

Chapter Sixteen
Aftermath

If the threat is real, it is not paranoia.

— Hsieh Tsung-Min (1934-)

The ecstasy of success was short-lived. At midweek, I learned from a board meeting at the Taipei Language Institute that the Investigative Bureau had begun asking questions about Judith and me three weeks earlier. "Was one of us on the board?" "Did we make policy at the school?" "Where did we live?"

As far as we were able to find out, the questions were prompted by our possible connection to a Taiwanese teacher named Wei (not T'ing-chao) at the school who was running for a local office as a nonparty (non-KMT) candidate. He had resisted government pressure to withdraw from the race. The director of the school had been under pressure to fire another Taiwanese teacher, George Wu, because of his friendship with Wei, and they had attempted to get Wei's wife fired from her job as a primary school teacher. Judith had introduced Wei to Fox before he left for New York, and he had written an article about him in the *New York Times*. The Investigative Bureau wanted to know who had arranged the contact. Because of the bad publicity the article generated internationally, the bureau didn't want the school to fire Wei himself, and they released his father, whom they had arrested to pressure Wei out of the race.

We later learned that the bureau had settled on Jerry Fowler as the culprit. We were acquainted with Jerry because he was married to Sue, who helped arrange Richard's adoption. In 1967, when we were going through the adoption screening process with Sue, we invited them to dinner at our house. Peter had heard that Fowler was on the staff at the U.S. Embassy and thought it might be good to meet him, so we also invited Peter. We later came to suspect that he was in the CIA and kept our distance. Since Fowler was the second secretary in the political section of the U.S. Embassy, there wasn't much the bureau could do if they thought he had tipped off the reporter.

The news that the Investigative Bureau was asking questions about us was disquieting, but in that same week we also received the news that our application for the renewal of our residency permit had been approved and would be good until the end of 1970. Had they known of our four-year relationship with Peter or our involvement in distributing funds to families of political prisoners, it is hard to imagine that they would have renewed the permit. Refusing to renew the residency permit was the most frequent way the Foreign Affairs Police dealt with undesirable foreigners.

Wei T'ing-chao came to the house on Wednesday, January 6. He was excited to hear about what had happened. He didn't ask us how we knew or what role we had in the escape. And we didn't say.

On Sunday, January 11, I went south for one of my regular visits to Tainan. I was able to celebrate Peter's escape with Rowland and others there. They didn't know any details of the escape, and I didn't tell them.

I was back in Taipei on Thursday for my classes there and began catching up on some of my work as registrar. On Saturday, January 17, two conversations undermined whatever ease I felt about getting our residency permits renewed.

"Ah, Lau Meng," I said as I opened the kitchen door. "Welcome! I haven't seen you in a long time."

Lau Meng ("Old Meng") was a forty-year-old dissident Mainlander with a long beard and a perpetual broad smile who looked like what his ancient Chinese philosopher ancestor, Mencius, might have looked like. I hadn't seen Meng since the previous summer when he had been my Chinese tutor for several months. He glanced over his shoulder through the screen door that, despite the fact that it led into the kitchen, was the commonly used entrance to our house.

"I'm sorry it has been so long," he said, not following me into the living room. "I have not come sooner because friends had warned me that you and Judith were being watched."

"I don't blame you for not coming," I said. "Did they say anything more?"

"No, only that some security agency had taken an interest in you," he said. "I don't know which agency."

Lau Meng seemed anxious to leave. In the months when he had been my tutor he regularly stayed as if he had nothing else to do.

"Will you have a cup of coffee?" I asked. While Meng enjoyed coaching me on Chinese culture and manners, he was eager to learn about Western ways. I had learned that he didn't want tea when he came to the house, but coffee heavily laced with milk and sugar. When he came several times a week for Chinese lessons, he would often stay for lunch. While we ate mostly Chinese, we occasionally made hamburgers. The idea of eating raw onions is abhorrent to the tastes of most Chinese people, but Old Meng insisted on having raw onions because that's the way it was done in the United States.

"No, thank you," he said. "I must not stay here too long."

We said good-bye and he disappeared down the lane in front of the administration building and chapel to the bus stop beyond.

Meng had hardly gone when Lo I-jen knocked at the door. Rail thin with a full head of wavy black hair and thick horn-rimmed glasses, I-jen and his wife Lucy lived directly across the tiny lane from our house. Both had a Ph.D. from Princeton and had arrived back in Taiwan to take up teaching positions at the seminary about the same time I was appointed there. Their son, Teddy, was a little older than Elizabeth and they were best friends. I-jen taught the New Testament and also worked with the Bible Society on a new translation in Taiwanese. Lucy taught Christian education. Both had been born and raised in the

Taipei area. Now they were back from having lived in the States for five or six years. They were our best friends on the faculty.

"Have you got a few minutes?" I-jen said as he stood outside the screen door.

"Come on in," I said, still trying to process what I had heard from Lau Meng.

We worked closely together on every seminary matter. I assumed that I-jen was there to discuss the curriculum and graduation requirement revision that he, Lucy, Judith, and I were proposing to the faculty. He came in and sat down in his usual chair in the living room.

"I've got some bad news," he said. "When I was talking with David this morning about our proposal, he said that he had learned you were being watched."

"Being watched" was a chilling message to receive, far more so for a Taiwanese or even Mainlander than a foreigner because inside me there was the sense that the worst that would happen to me was deportation. Taiwanese had no such illusions. They knew that people disappeared with some regularity, many of whom were never heard from again. The message that one was "being watched" was an escalation of the experience of the White Terror that Taiwanese lived with daily. The fact that no foreign residents had disappeared did little to minimize the emotional impact of I-jen's words, which came only minutes after those of Lau Meng. I felt a physical chill run down my spine.

"How did David learn that?" I asked.

"He said that Chang Hsin-yi's father told him yesterday." Hsin-yi was one of my brightest students, and after graduating in June he would be off for graduate study at Boston University. His father was a prominent Presbyterian pastor in Taipei.

"Hsin-yi came to see me some weeks ago letting me know his suspicion that Bing Shr-jye was a paid informer for one of the secret police agencies," I said. Mr. Bing was a nonteaching staff person at the seminary. "Hsin-yi said that Bing has a brother who works for the Investigative Bureau, a brother who works for the Garrison Command,

and a sister who graduated from the Political College in Beito."

"I've always suspected Bing," I-jen said "and am careful what I say around him."

"Hsin-yi didn't say anything about my being of any concern to Bing or anyone else," I said, "and I think he would have if he knew."

"I can't say that I am surprised," I-jen said. "Since the government has started pressuring the church to withdraw from the World Council of Churches, I think several of us are under scrutiny because we've been advising David on this matter—you included."

Was that all that had attracted attention to me? I wished that I could have talked with I-jen about what other things there might be, including Peter's escape, but I didn't.

Five days later, on January 22, we received our first letter from Peter. Jim Brentlinger brought it from Hong Kong. Peter reported that he had gotten to Sweden around midnight on January 4. When changing planes in Copenhagen, before the last leg of his trip, he sent telegrams to Bud in Hong Kong and to the people in Japan.

Before landing in Stockholm, Peter said he went to the restroom, tore up his forged passport, and flushed it down the commode so that he could not be charged with traveling with false documents. When he disembarked, someone from Amnesty International who had been notified of his coming met him. He declared himself a person without papers and requested asylum. There would be no announcement of his escape or presence in Sweden until asylum was formally granted.

On Sunday, Abe had gone to the Japanese Embassy in Taipei and reported that he had lost his passport. They said to come back on Monday to get his new papers. Peter expected to hear from Abe as soon as he got back to Japan. When a week went by and he heard nothing, Peter was frantic with worry that something had happened or that Abe had been arrested. After two weeks of worry in Stockholm, the word finally came that Abe had returned. After receiving his new papers on January 4, Abe decided to extend his "vacation" and visit the Philippines before going home.

Peter also reported that DeWitt's seat on the plane was one row behind his on the other side. When Peter boarded, DeWitt was in his seat. Their eyes met and DeWitt offered a half smile of recognition and then looked back down at the magazine he was holding. When the plane landed in Hong Kong, by prearrangement they did not speak or celebrate. DeWitt went his way, and Peter found Bud waiting for him.

Exactly when the authorities in Taiwan realized that Peter had escaped is not clear. The day after we received Peter's letter, when he had been out of the country for twenty days, Mr. Yén called and we invited him to dinner. Over two years earlier, Peter had introduced us to Yén Gèn-Chāng, head of the Taipei printers' union. Mr. Yén had a storied reputation. He had been head of the union over twenty years earlier during 2-28. The union was so strong that they surrounded the union headquarters when the Nationalist soldiers were indiscriminately killing throughout the city, and the soldiers backed down. Years later, Mr. Yén was elected to the National Assembly. He was short and balding and always wore gold-rimed glasses. He drank too much.

He was full of sayings and always had a new one for us when we were with him.

"When you see someone on the street, can you tell if he is a Taiwanese or a Mainlander?" he once asked me.

"Can you tell by the way they speak?" I asked.

"No, you can tell before you talk to them. If they are standing up straight, you know they are Mainlanders. Taiwanese are all a little bent over," he said, demonstrating with his posture and his head bent down. "It is a physical condition resulting from all the bowing and scraping they have done in the presence of the Mainlanders over the years," Mr. Yén said, laughing at himself and his own people.

"Do you know how to tell the difference between a rich man and a poor man?" he asked on another occasion.

"No, I don't know," I said, preparing for another lesson.

"Because the rich have more money, they eat more and so have to spend more time on the commode. Rich people shit more; that's the difference between them and poor people."

Mr. Yén didn't have any wise sayings tonight. He had a more serious demeanor than that to which we were accustomed. At dinner, he reported a conversation he had had with a Chinese newspaper reporter in the afternoon.

"The reporter said that Peng was in America!"

"He couldn't be serious," Judith said.

"The KMT has issued a denial, saying that Peng is in Taiwan, but I think they are blowing smoke," he responded. "I went directly to Peng's house and asked Mrs. Peng. She said that two men from the Investigative Bureau had come at three o'clock and asked where Peng was. Then, they informed her that he was in America. No sooner had they gone than a *New York Times* reporter and someone from the Associated Press came asking the same thing. I told her I was going to come to see if you had heard anything. She didn't say not to come, but she said to make sure I wasn't followed."

"Were you followed?" I asked.

"Yes, but I lost them by changing taxis a couple of times. Cost me about $180 NT to get here," he said with a laugh.

"We haven't heard anything," I said. "We haven't heard from him in a few weeks and thought he had gone to Kaohsiung to visit his mother."

"I don't think the United States would welcome him," Judith said.

"Do you think it is possible that he has been arrested and that this is the government's cover story?" I asked.

"I don't think so," Mr. Yén said, seemingly thinking about the possibility. "I think he's gone, and if he is, I say good for him. Let's drink a toast!"

"We don't have any alcohol," I said. "I guess we'll have to celebrate with coffee."

Peng's escape created a nightmare of public relations for Chiang's government. They denied that he was gone and had egg on their faces when they learned that the rest of the world knew it before they did. They compounded the problem when they changed their story; the date they said he had escaped was three weeks after the actual event.

When we met Wei T'ing-chao to give him funds for the families that had come in, he filled us in on what was happening behind the scenes.

"They didn't believe Peng was gone because the security team assigned to follow him had been submitting expense vouchers for following him all around the island during the weeks when he was in fact already gone."

"I guess Ching-kuo and his daddy weren't amused by their security team, were they?" I said, almost giggling.

"When they learned that the team filed false expense vouchers for these three weeks, it didn't take long—using their usual methods—for the guards to confess that there were weeks and months when they hadn't seen Dr. Peng but continued filling out false reports about following him. None of this, of course, has been reported publicly. It would be too embarrassing for the government."

"Do you know what's happened to those in charge?"

"Many senior officers in the Investigative Bureau lost their jobs. The department chief who had so viciously threatened Dr. Peng became the scapegoat and is already in prison."

"What about the guards who filed the false reports?"

"They are missing," Wei said.

The government finally had to acknowledge the escape and allowed the newspapers to run small stories about it suggesting that he had escaped with the assistance of the CIA. That seemed reasonable to many because they couldn't imagine how anyone could escape from the island without the aid of such an agency. Peter, of course, insisted that he had not received any government aid except when he was received in Sweden.[17] And he was telling the truth. It still tickles me when I think about it.

What the government knew about Judith and me or how interested they were in us was not clear. We speculated that they didn't know a lot about our relationship with Peter, our connection with the aid going to political prisoners' families, or Peter's escape. We imagined that there were many more likely points that would have been brought to their attention: the situation at the language school, my reports to Principal Chen on the pressure for the PCT to withdraw from the world council, lectures in my ecumenics class when I addressed the issue of the WCC, reports about my feelings about the political situation generally from informers at the seminary or elsewhere, or public contacts with Yen and other dissident Taiwanese. Any or all of these would have been sufficient to attract the attention of security agencies.

Almost daily, I wondered if I was being paranoid about the importance of the reports that I was "being watched." I shared this with Hsieh Tsung-min the next time I met him. Hsieh was still gaunt and thin from his years in prison, which made his bushy eyebrows stand out even more than usual.

"Thousands of people are being watched all of the time, aren't they?" I said.

"Yes," he said, "but some are watched more than others," a phrase reminiscent of a statement in *Animal Farm* about some pigs "being more equal than others." If I hadn't been fairly certain Hsieh had not read the book, I might have thought he was making a pun.

"Wei and I are now watched twenty-four hours a day since Dr. Peng escaped. They can't believe that we didn't have something to do with it," he said. And, as if to

---

[17] In *A Taste of Freedom* (1972) Peter wrote this:
"Unfortunately since so many people were involved, I am still unable to explain how I escaped without endangering those brave and loyal friends. I can say, however, that I have received no help from any government except, of course, the Swedish government which gave me political asylum." (p. 219)

reassure me, he added, "They are not any better at following us than they were with Dr. Peng."

"I am not surprised that you have more attention. Judith and I have had several reports within the past weeks of being watched."

"There is a way you can tell how your mail is being checked," he said. "I met a man in prison who used to work for the postal security branch. He had stolen money from letters and had been caught. He explained to me the postal code on the cancellation stamp on every letter that is mailed in Taiwan. From it, you can tell if your letter was checked."

"Wow!" was all I could say. "And you know this code?"

"Yes," he said. "It's easy."

He pulled a piece of paper out of his jacket and sketched the cancellation stamp on the back.

"You can see the post office where the letter was processed. The date and hour is a way to keep track of the postal employee who processed your letter so that he or she can be held accountable if they let something important get through."

Then he pointed to the parenthesis at the bottom of the stamp with a single character inside.

"There are three different characters that can be in this parenthesis," he said as he wrote. "This character means that the letter wasn't checked. This character means that it was checked by the postal security system. And this character means that it was checked by the Garrison Command. If you start receiving many letters with that character, you know they are really interested in you. All of the mail I receive has the Garrison Command character on it."

Hsieh handed me the piece of paper and I tucked it into my billfold.

"Thanks!" I said twice as we parted, in awe of what Hsieh and Wei had been able to learn while they were behind bars but also a little fearful about the piece of paper in my billfold. Although we didn't use the mail system for any sensitive matters, I wondered at what level my mail was being checked.

As soon as I got back to the seminary, I went in to the office where the day's mail was spread out on a desk for people to pick up. As I went through the pieces looking for ones addressed to me, I looked at the cancellation stamp on different letters. Most had the "not checked" character in the parenthesis, and a few had the "postal security" check. I didn't receive any mail on that day. But over the next few days, when I received letters, none of them had the "not checked" character. Several of them had the "postal security" character, and a couple of them had the "Garrison Command" character. Over the coming weeks, more of my letters had that mark on them.

I thought about what Hsieh had said about some "being watched more than others" and his last words that day before we parted.

"If the threat is real," he had said, "it is not paranoia."

Chapter Seventeen
What Would Jesus Do?

I want to join the Freedom Fighters but my religion worries me. Can a Christian take up guns and sticks against his fellow man?

—Daniel M. N. in a letter to Colin Morris (1969)

In the wake of the violence inspired by religious faith in the 9/11 attacks and how, at least in less xenophobic minds, the memory of Christianity's blessing of violence in earlier centuries has been painfully recalled, I raise the question of a Christian's legitimating violence in the pursuit of justice with some reluctance. However much one may recoil at the notion of religion-inspired violence serving just ends, are we not compelled to admit that the acquiescence of religious people to state-sponsored violence, whether in the case of the Vietnam War or the U.S. invasion of Iraq, constitute de facto legitimizations of its use? Niebuhr's dictum of 1932—"once the factor of coercion is ethically justified... we cannot draw any absolute line of demarcation between violent and nonviolent coercion"[18]—seemed particularly apt as the events of 1970 unfolded.

Even before Peter's escape, we had been rethinking our furlough plans. Our original arrangement with the board of missions was to serve five years in Taiwan and then take a year's furlough in which I could complete my dissertation. In the fall of 1969 and the spring of 1970, two things happened to change that plan. Having what we believed to be reliable information that we had gotten the attention of the government and were sometimes actually being watched, we believed that if we left the country for a year

---

[18] *Moral Man and Immoral Society*, p. 131.

and had to apply again for a new residency permit that we would not be allowed back into the country.

Our current residency permits would not expire until December 1970. We decided to request a three-month furlough in the summer of 1970 and return for a three-year term, after which time we would take a full year and do my dissertation. Since I had completed my residency requirements and exams at Boston University in the spring of 1965, I was pushing the time limit I had to complete my dissertation. BU agreed to extend the time for me according to the schedule I proposed.

We considered not leaving Taiwan at all, but that possibility was preempted by the need to get Richard naturalized as an American citizen. We could not do it from outside the country. Getting the adoption done in Taiwan was not a problem for the government there, but it had been a problem for the officials at the U.S. Consulate. Because they gave us such a hard time about the way Richard had come to the home in Taichung, we didn't know if we would encounter difficulties in the U.S. We just knew that we needed to get him there and naturalized.

Having a current residency permit would not keep the government from refusing us reentry after three months outside nor would it keep us in the country if the government decided it didn't want us there. At this point, however, we didn't know what the government really knew about us, so we decided on the three-month furlough.

What would happen to the distribution of funds to families of political prisoners during the summer? Hsieh and Wei needed a contact to pass them the funds that came in through Hong Kong. We didn't want to risk having Hsieh or Wei in direct contact with whoever the courier might be. The Hoovers and Heaths would have been happy to do the job, but they were completing their year of language school and scheduled to assume their responsibilities in Singapore and Sarawak that summer. We decided to recruit a missionary couple who had not been involved in anything else we had done.

In March we approached Carlisle and Ruth Phillips. Carlisle and Ruth had been in Taiwan since long before I arrived; before that they had been among the last missionaries to leave the China Mainland after the Chinese Communists took power and had had some time under house arrest before leaving China. Their work in Taiwan had been with Mainlanders in the Methodist Church of Taiwan and, at the time, Carlisle was the pastor of a Methodist Church in Taipei. However, unlike most of the "old China hands" that I knew in Taiwan, the Phillipses were sympathetic to the Taiwanese. They were also people I thought I could ask who, even if they said no, would not betray me or the work I was asking them to do.

Over lunch at a small dumpling restaurant, we explained what we were doing with Hsieh and Wei (and that for security reasons we now referred to them as "Tony" and "Matthew") with families of political prisoners and our need to go back to the States for three months.

"We need for you to be the liaison between couriers bringing in the money—most of the time the courier will be Jim Brentlinger—and Tony and Matthew," I said. "Your meetings will have to be secret, but both of them are good at not being followed."

"Of course we will do it," Ruth said without waiting for Carlisle to respond. Her hair prematurely gray, Ruth always seemed to have a smile on her face and a twinkle in her eye. Carlisle was regarded as a bit eccentric; he rarely looked at you when talking. He usually took a little time before answering any question, but I had learned to pay attention when he spoke. After a few moments of silence, he nodded in agreement with Ruth.

"When do we get to meet the two young men?" Ruth said.

Their immediate agreement had surprised me. I heaved a sigh of relief knowing that the program could continue without interruption through the summer of 1970.

"It is possible," Judith said, breaking the gaiety of the moment, "that we will not be allowed back into the country in September. In that case, you will have to decide whether or not to continue."

"If it becomes necessary," Ruth said, "we'll decide. But we are not quitters."

Even though we had been reading about the polarization of the U.S. over the war in Vietnam, not physically being in the country limited our sense of what was happening. We had also been preoccupied with our own issues in Taiwan. When George Todd, then an executive with the United Presbyterian Board of National Missions in New York, heard that we were coming on furlough, he insisted that we spend significant time and energy learning what was happening at home. The expectations of our own board of missions were that we visit our supporting church in Fort Worth, be available for speaking engagements, and rest. Around the schedule arranged by the Methodists, Todd set up an itinerary and contacts for us from California to New York.

The wisdom of Todd's counsel became even more apparent as events unfolded in the months before we left Taiwan. In December of 1969, the first draft lottery since World War II was instituted. In February the mass murder of hundreds of unarmed civilians by U.S. Army Forces at My Lai and My Khe was confirmed. In March, the U.S. began bombing North Vietnamese sanctuaries and supply routes in Cambodia. In April, U.S. and Vietnamese troops invaded Cambodia. News of the massacre and the expansion of the war into Cambodia prompted unprecedented outrage from many parts of the world. Unable to manipulate public opinion at home, it looked like Nixon was losing control.

Nixon decided to see if any kind of rapprochement with Mao Tse-tung and the Chinese Communists was possible. In January of 1970 a spokesperson for the U.S. State Department referred for the first time to the "People's Republic of China," instead of the usual "Red China" or "Communist China." The language was a signal to Beijing, and it wasn't missed there or in Taipei, nor was the State Department's announcement of the easing of travel restrictions to China in March. In April, Chiang Ching-kuo came to the U.S. to make the case for the Nationalists.

The son of Chiang Kai-shek, Ching-kuo spent twelve years in the Soviet Union and married a Russian woman, who returned to China with him in 1937. When the Nationalists retreated to Taiwan after the loss of the Mainland, Chiang appointed his son head of the hydra-headed secret police agencies. Given Ching-kuo's background, modeling the Nationalist security agencies on Stalin's was not surprising. To the Chiang family's anti-Communist supporters in the United States, it was a reality unknown or conveniently ignored. In Taiwan, Ching-kuo's name invoked fear—fear for the White Terror he directed, as well as fear that he might readily cut a deal with the Chinese Communists rather than allow the Taiwanese to shape the future of their island nation.

The KMT was not the only party concerned about Nixon's overtures to the People's Republic. Advocates for an independent Taiwan were also concerned. In early 1970, the World United Formosans for Independence (WUFI) was organized to coordinate the efforts of a myriad of groups advocating Taiwanese independence. Operating out of the haven of other countries, Ching-kuo's visit was made-to-order for protest. WUFI organized demonstrations against him wherever he went in New York City.

On April 24, twenty-five protesters gathered outside the Plaza Hotel where "Little Chiang," as he was not affectionately known in Taiwan, was slated to address a luncheon meeting of the Far East-American Council of Commerce and Industry. As he walked through the revolving door at the Plaza, WUFI member Peter Ng pulled a pistol out of his raincoat, ran forward, and pointed it at Ching-kuo. New York Detective James Ziede, part of the detail to protect Chiang, saw Ng and grabbed his arm. The shot hit the glass door but not the vice premier. Ng's brother-in-law, T.T. Deh, was also arrested in the struggle as Ng shouted, "Let me stand up like a Taiwanese!" Both men claimed to be members of the WUFI.

Had it not been for the fact that the United States was ablaze with controversy over the Vietnam War, the assassination attempt might have been bigger news. But ten days later, when four students were killed in an antiwar demonstration at Kent State by members of the Ohio National Guard on May 4, little more was heard about the incident at the hotel. Within five days of the shootings at Kent State, over one hundred thousand held demonstrations in Washington D.C. Windows were smashed, tires were slashed, and fires were set. Nixon's chief speechwriter, Ray Price, said, "That's not student protest. That's civil war." Nixon himself was removed to Camp David for his safety for two days. The Eighty-second Airborne was installed in the basement of the executive office building. Four million students protested or went on strike. Nine hundred universities were closed because of violent and nonviolent demonstrations. The U.S. was culturally and politically polarized to a degree not known since the Civil War.

In a country that many thought was on the brink of civil war, the point was lost on most that the attempt on Ching-kuo's life was the first high-profile incident of violent resistance by the Taiwanese to Chiang's Nationalist government since he had retreated to Taiwan in 1949.

Mr. Yén, our friend and the head of the printers' union, had a ready explanation for the failure: "The Taiwanese do not know how to fight; they don't know the first thing about using guns." While the story was quickly relegated to the back pages in the United States, shock waves of even tighter government control rippled across Taiwan.

I was not altogether surprised when I received a letter through Hong Kong from a friend in the U.S. who suggested in an almost offhand way that since Nixon seemed to be moving toward rapprochement with the People's Republic, what was needed in Taiwan was "a bloody incident" that would call attention to the situation.

"That's a damned easy thing for him to say," I said to Judith as I read the letter to her. "He's not here."

"Nor is he Taiwanese," she added.

The next time I saw Tony, I shared the letter with him.

"Dr. Peng used to say that people outside were always quick to suggest the shedding of our blood," he said with a laugh.

I don't think the friend was suggesting that we orchestrate an incident, but rather observing what he thought would be required to mobilize world opinion. He was not alone in his suggestion that violence was necessary in responding to violent regimes. During that spring, I ordered a book that had been published in 1969 by Abingdon, our denominational press. The author, Colin Morris, was a part-time British Methodist missionary and part-time advisor to Kenneth Kaunda, President of the Republic of Zambia (formerly Northern Rhodesia). Morris' book[19] was written in response to a question about whether a Christian could take up arms in Africa's anticolonial struggle.

Yes was Morris' unequivocal reply. The world, he said, is ruled by the unyoung, uncolored, and unpoor; only violent revolution could overthrow them and provide a decent future for the majority of the world's population. Christians, Morris argued, have both the right and responsibility to take part in this struggle. I was surprised and pleased to see the question so important for me was being addressed by a fellow missionary and that my own denomination's press saw fit to publish it.

In the chapter "The Sacred Cow of Nonviolence," Morris said,

> Passive resistance depends for its success upon the creation of public opinion which will be shamed or angered into giving justice to those who choose to match official power with self-sacrifice...
>
> Ruthless modern despots do not play good-natured games with their critics. It is hard to imagine Hitler or Stalin blanching at the prospect of Gandhi fasting to death. They would have helped him on his way, exterminating him secretly so that there was no mark of his passing except for a bloodstain on some

---

[19] Colin Morris, *Unyoung Uncolored Unpoor* (Nashville: Abingdon Press, 1969).

cellar wall... People who vanish without a trace do not make effective rallying points for freedom..[20]

Morris was saying what Peter had said and what I had concluded about the efficacy of nonviolent resistance in Taiwan. But as I read on, I wished for Peter's presence to discuss with him what Morris said was determinative for him: "As a Christian writing to another Christian, my argument stands or falls by [Jesus'] attitude to violence."[21]

In the chapter "What Would Jesus Do," Morris makes the proper caveats about what we don't know about the historical Jesus but reminds the reader that in spite of the claims made about him as an advocate of nonviolence, the one thing corroborated about him by the non-Christian historians of his time was that he was executed for the crime of sedition against the Roman government. The Gospels attempt to prove the charge false, and that has become the commonly accepted Christian interpretation. Not so for Morris:

> The Gospel portrait of Jesus is comparable to a biography of a German churchman of the 1930s which makes no mention of his attitude toward the Nazis... If Jesus was oblivious of all the violence around him, or regarded it as unimportant, then our efforts to make him relevant to the life of our time are futile because he was irrelevant to his own time. And what is more, he was a dangerous, blundering fool, doing ambiguous acts and saying provocative things that invited bloody retaliation upon his followers, all the while protesting that he was being misunderstood. [22]

While Morris was speaking to questions that I had had since the seminary, I learned that he had help. As he was struggling to make sense of Jesus and violence, he learned

---

[20] Morris, pp. 86-87.
[21] Morris, p. 83
[22] Morris, p. 102.

of S. G. F. Brandon's book *Jesus and the Zealots*, published while Morris was working on his book.[23]

I ordered Brandon's book at once and read it during the spring of 1970. Brandon was a well-respected specialist in New Testament background, at least until he published this tome. In painstaking detail he documented how Palestine was aflame with the guerilla war waged by Zealots against the Romans during Jesus' lifetime and how there are only oblique clues in the Gospels to what was happening. He argued that since Mark, the presumed first Gospel, was written in Rome as the Jewish War was reaching its climax, Christians were especially vulnerable because of Jesus' execution on the charge of sedition. Their lives could have depended on Mark's showing Jesus' death was a tragic mistake. The explanation, became the orthodox view of the Christian Church.

Examining in great detail such incidents as Jesus' triumphal entry to Jerusalem, his encounter with the money changers in the temple, and his response on taxation convinced Brandon that Jesus, while not a Zealot, was likely sympathic to their cause to free their country from Roman control.

I came to see that the attempt to present Jesus not as a threat to Rome was a reasonable act of self-preservation for the early church. I saw similar writing in the Presbyterian Church of Taiwan. As a Taiwanese church, they were always suspected by the government and under the threat of persecution. Their newsletters had a kind of doublespeak about all things political, but in a code that the people understood. I'm not sure but that was true in the earliest church and in the Gospels.

Brandon's meticulous work validated questions I had about the Jesus of the Gospels and changed forever the way I looked the major events of Jesus' life. This was no idle theological speculation; like Morris, my stance for what I was prepared to do in Taiwan was dependent on what I believed Jesus' attitude toward violence was. While I

---

[23] S. G. F. Brandon, *Jesus and the Zealots: A Study of the Political Factor in Primitive Christianity* (Manchester: Manchester University Press, 1967).

agreed with Brandon that Jesus may have been sympathetic to the attempt to throw off Rome, I decided that Jesus' association with tax collectors and his refusal to restrict God's grace to the Jewish people would have put him at odds with the Zealots. Jesus' mission, I concluded, included but was not limited to the struggle with Rome.

While I didn't share Morris' emphatic yes to the use of violence to fight against injustice, I lost forever the Gospel's presumption of the pacifist Jesus. A pacifist he might have been, but he might also have assumed that when he came to Jerusalem to confront the religious and political authorities that the people would rise up and throw out the Romans as the people had thrown out the Greeks two hundred years earlier. Or, he might have believed in that confrontation God would unleash legions of angel armies that would come down from the clouds and vanquish the Romans. Or, despite Gospel claims to the contrary, I came to suspect he came to confront the authorities not sure what would happen, knowing only that he was doing the right thing as he understood it and that in all likelihood it would cost him his life.

I prepared to leave Taiwan for three months no longer assuming that Jesus had to be a pacifist. If I were allowed to return to Taiwan in September, I would have to decide what that meant for my work there.

The primary objective of the trip home was to complete the process of making Richard a naturalized U.S. citizen. The secondary objective was to visit our supporting church —First United Methodist Church in Fort Worth. This church had assumed our full support. Another objective was to try to learn what was going on in the United States. To that end, George Todd scheduled visits for us with people and groups from Berkley to New York City.

George wanted us to have a sense of the antiwar movement from the people in it. A meeting in Berkley had been arranged with a group of activists who had disrupted the 1968 Methodist General Conference with an antiwar demonstration. We were staying in a hotel in downtown San Francisco and were given directions to drive across the

Bay Bridge to a house in Berkeley. With Elizabeth, who had turned four in April, and Richard, who wouldn't be two until the next October, we set out in a rented car to find the house. The house was old and run-down in an old and run-down neighborhood. We were welcomed by about ten or fifteen young women and men sitting around a living room with only pillows on the floor. Some of them may have had earlier church connections, but I sensed that most had not and were organized to challenge the religious institutions. The person who had arranged our meeting had provided us with sufficient credibility that we were warmly welcomed. After we had been there for a while, one of the men opened a bag of what he said was peyote that he had gotten from Native Americans in Colorado a week or so before. I didn't know what peyote was. They stuffed it into a pipe, lit it and passed it around the circle. Since I had been smoking my own pipe with tobacco since we got there, I declined. Judith thought it impolite, but I didn't reconsider. The gathered folks seemed not to be offended by my lack of participation. Within the next hour or so our hosts began to fall asleep right on the floor where we were sitting. Finally, when everyone had gone to sleep but us, we gathered up Richard and Liz and returned to our hotel.

In New York City, Todd had arranged for us to meet with a group of returned Peace Corps Volunteers. We met this group on the Upper West Side of Manhattan. I found much in common with these young people. They had been politicized by their experiences outside the U.S. like I had been in Taiwan. They were vigorously antiwar, but not as strident as other groups we met.

Todd had even arranged a meeting with the Black Panthers. In a slum section on the Lower East Side we found our way to an upstairs apartment where we met with two of the leaders of the movement in New York City. Again, our friend had given us sufficient introductions so that we weren't met with overt hostility, which was pretty much the way Black Panthers viewed Anglos. That we were able to have such a meeting at all was testimony to the credibility George Todd—who was also Anglo—had with them. In low-key tones, as if we might be discussing directions to get back to our hotel, they dismissed the nonviolent approach of Dr. King and the Civil Rights movement and said that the use of force was the only way for black survival. They admitted that since the authorities had vast superiority in firepower, their ability to protect blacks was limited.

The strangest meeting of the summer was with Peter Ng and T.T. Deh, the two would-be assassins of Chiang Ching-kuo. Our meeting was only a month or two after the attempt they made on Chiang's life. They were out on bail, made possible by many Taiwanese living in the U.S. putting up their homes as collateral. We had never met nor heard of either man before the assassination attempt. T.T. was then secretary general of the World United Formosans for Independence (WUFI) in the United States. Peter Ng was a thrity-three-year-old doctoral student at Cornell University. Ng was the one who fired the shots supposedly because he was single, while Deh had a wife and two children.

Since they couldn't talk about anything related to the attempt or their upcoming trial, we soon ran out of things to discuss.[24] In retrospect, the decision to meet them at all seems foolish. The risk of the meeting becoming known to U.S. or Taiwanese authorities seemed hardly worth any other value it might have had. I may have agreed to the meeting because I wanted to meet and take the measure of the first two Taiwanese to "take up arms" against Chiang's government.

---

[24] Before they could be tried in 1971, they disappeared, causing all the Taiwanese who had put up money and a number who had used their homes as collateral to be left holding the bag. Needless to say, Ng and Deh were not popular in the expatriate Taiwanese community. Deh fled to Sweden but was extradited back to the U.S. and served twenty-two months for his part in the crime. Ng disappeared for more than twenty years and only showed up in Taiwan in 2000 because his mother was dying. He was tried for illegal entry and spent a year in jail.

The main purpose of the furlough had been Richard's naturalization. Once accomplished, we boarded a flight in Dallas to return to Taiwan in time for the beginning of the fall semester at the seminary. Less clear was what I learned from our summer, except that there was a national atmosphere of animosity and a willingness to embrace violence unlike anything I had known. I was now less judgmental about those who chose violence to resist the war in Vietnam, Black Panthers to protect black communities, or Taiwanese to resist Chiang's oppression. What Jesus might have done in his time mattered to me, but at the end of the summer I had to admit that I was on my own. Ethically, Colin Morris' counsel to the young man in Africa made sense to me, and the Nationalist regime in Taiwan was no less brutal or intractable than the colonial governments in Africa. Although the innocent were suffering already, I knew I could not be party to violence in which more innocents would suffer. Besides, I couldn't imagine any such act that would do a bit of good. Was my stance shaped in any way by a fear of consequences for me or my family? If that fear had the upper hand, I wouldn't have done many of the things I had already done. Despite Niebuhr's dictum that the line between violence and nonviolence was not absolute, I sensed a personal chasm between them, one that if I crossed I would no longer be who I thought I was. I was also convinced that my Taiwanese friends—who seemed immune to fear—resisted the use of violence because they didn't want to increase the suffering of innocent people and couldn't see any positive outcome of such acts.

I had no idea what lay before us in Taiwan, but as we landed at Taipei International Airport, I had a strong feeling that we would not spend another three years there.

Chapter Eighteen
The Closing Net

You have only the power to act;
You do not have power to determine the result;
So act without anticipation of the result;
And not succumb to inaction.

—Krishna in the *Bhagavad Gita*

As soon as we returned to Taipei in September, I met with the Phillipses to see how the distribution of funds to the families had gone. Carlisle kept careful records of all the money that came in and that they turned over to Hsieh and Wei, who had in turn distributed it. I was pleased to find that the foursome not only worked well together but seemed to have developed genuine affection for one other. Ruth talked about "the boys" as if they were family.

Although we met with Matthew and Tony regularly, it was always separately. All of us getting together seemed to be an unnecessary risk. Even though the two of them stayed in constant touch with each other, it was frustrating not to be able to talk with both of them at the same time. That wasn't new. Even before Peter escaped, I don't recall a time when the three of them were together with us or a time when Matthew and Tony were together with us. At different times in our relationship, all three had separately acted as my tutors in Chinese, helping me with my history lectures.

Looking at the mail that had accumulated for us in our absence, I could see from the postmark codes that more and more letters were making stops at the Garrison Command before arriving in our mailbox. Within weeks of our getting back, there were new reports that we were being watched. By which agency or for what reasons, we had no idea.

In separate conversations, I asked Matthew and Tony if they thought it wise for them to continue distributing money. Tony answered by describing the great need of prisoners' families for even the little bits of money he could put in their hands.

"We can distribute the money without the KMT knowing that we are the ones doing it," Tony said. "The larger problem is finding the families who are always on the move. Getting money to them is critical, and Wei and I are the only ones who can do it."

Left unsaid by Tony was the danger of families reporting him out of fear. He and Matthew had both encountered people in desperate need but too fearful to accept money. If the government used their usual means to get someone to talk, both Tony and Matthew were at risk.

"What are they going to do to us—put us in prison?" Matthew responded with a laugh when I asked him the same question. Not easily intimidated, eighteen years earlier when in his second year at Cheng-kong High School in Taipei he refused to join the Youth Anti-Communist National Salvation Corps (known popularly as the China Youth Corps and modeled on the China Youth League in the People's Republic), quit school, and began tutoring illiterate children who were learning to read. Without a high school diploma, he took the university entrance exam, passed it, and entered the Department of Law at the National University. By late 1970, when we had the conversation, Matthew knew well what prison was like. He had challenged his guards to shoot him and challenged the court that sentenced him to give him the death penalty. He wouldn't even entertain the question of stopping the distribution.

Carlisle turned his notebook with records of receipts and disbursements over to me. As soon as I got home, I destroyed it. I wanted no paper that could incriminate them, Matthew, or Tony. I also decided that I could no longer afford the luxury of keeping a journal. I did not consider destroying the trunk full of collated and stapled articles that we continued to give to foreign visitors. That would come later.

We quickly settled into a surreal normalcy. The board of missions was moving ahead with its new policy of distancing itself from the Methodist Church in Taiwan, a policy I wholeheartedly endorsed. In addition to teaching my classes and doing my work as registrar, I was also involved in the now-approved major restructuring of the curriculum as well as negotiating team to merge the two seminaries, a merger that was foundering on the rivalry between the northern and southern Presbyterians.

I mused about two questions. First, how was it possible to live and work as a missionary, a seminary teacher and administrator while wondering when I would be arrested? I now had some sense of what it was to live two different lives. Thankfully, there were some missionary friends who knew at least part of my two lives, and when we were together, I didn't have to pretend to be one or the other.

The second question was why the government allowed us back into the country after the furlough. Given what some in the government must have suspected, it is a marvel that they allowed us back into the country. Perhaps the competition between the different security agencies— the Foreign Affairs Police, the Investigative Bureau, and the Garrison Command—kept them from sharing what information they had. What I had learned from my Taiwanese friends was that the KMT's system of fear-inducing brutality exercised through multiple security agencies was at the same time a tangle of corruption that guaranteed inefficiency. The question for me, though, was not if I would ever be found out and arrested, only when.

As I resumed my duties at the seminary, I felt a growing sense of sadness that at some point this would end. I loved teaching and when I arrived in Taiwan in 1965, I could think of no better future than teaching in this place. I knew there was no turning back.

Another part of the sadness, however, had little to do with politics. I knew that as long as the board of missions paid my salary, the seminary didn't have to hire or train a Taiwanese who could do my teaching job much more effectively than I could. My presence without costing the seminary anything except housing was a barrier to that important step being taken. At the same time I realized that what I had been doing politically were things that only I could do at a relatively minimal risk.

In the midst of this double life were Elizabeth and Richard. When we returned to Taiwan in September, Elizabeth was four and Richard was one. Elizabeth was in Chinese kindergarten at Mu-Ai Tang (Church of the Good Shepherd in Shih-lin). Her best friend was Teddy Loh, who lived across the road from us at the seminary and whose parents were my best friends at the seminary. Elizabeth was fluent in both Taiwanese (from her friends at the seminary) and in Mandarin (from her nursery school). Judith and I spoke only English to her so she wouldn't have bad models in Mandarin. Richard had such a calm disposition that I regularly put him in a backpack baby seat and did my work in the study. He would sleep there, but if he was awake, he would quietly amuse himself.

Although in the history of parents who adopt children not at all exceptional, in September we were surprised to learn that Judith was pregnant. We were delighted but fearful because the doctor told us that bearing another child was a considerable health risk. We were not sure that she could carry the baby to term. As fall gave way to winter, Judith passed the early critical periods.

One day in the fall, Mr. Yén called and invited us to dinner at a downtown restaurant with him and two guests from Japan. He said he would be grateful if we would help him entertain them. Except for the Japanese guests, the invitation was not unusual; he often invited us out to eat. Mr. Yén was always entertaining and sometimes a source for news from inside the government.

The evening was unremarkable. We met Mr. Yén and the two men in one of Taipei's many Japanese restaurants. The men were dressed in suits and ties and looked to be in their thirties or forties. We went through the usual drinking ritual toasting each other with sake. Mr. Yén interpreted the conversation for us in Mandarin. The conversation went from the tourist sites they were visiting to the speculation that the U.S. was moving closer to an attempt at establishing diplomatic relations with the People's Republic. When the tea was served, signaling the end of the evening, we shook hands, caught a taxi, and went home. Only in retrospect several months later would we suspect that the purpose of the meeting might have been more than we imagined.

Tensions within the KMT about Nixon's overtures to China reached a fevered pitch when, on October 5, 1970, President Nixon was quoted in *Time*, regarded as the most pro-KMT magazine in the United States: "If there is anything I want to do before I die, it is to go to China." To the Chiangs, Nixon was groveling in order to get an invitation to visit China. A week later on October 12, the library at the United States Information Agency in Tainan was bombed. No one was hurt and little damage to the building was done. News reports in Taiwan suggested that it was the result of widespread unhappiness with the United States. When we read the story, we laughed. The only "widespread unhappiness" with the U.S. in Taiwan we could see was the near hysteria within the government. We assumed that the bombing had been staged by the KMT. When Bank of America was bombed in Taipei on February 5, 1971, we made the same assumption.

On Thursday, February 18, 1971, we received a call from Mr. Yén, member of the National Assembly and head of the Taipei printers' union. He said that one of the two Japanese men we had helped him entertain, a man named Abe, was back in town and had a gift for us. Since we had only been guests at a dinner with them and had not discussed any of our activities, we couldn't imagine why one would be bringing us a gift. We speculated that they might be part of the independence movement based in Japan and perhaps had been part of facilitating the Japanese end of Peng's escape a year earlier. We didn't know that, nor did we know whether Peng had sent them to us. We assumed that this was merely an act of Asian hospitality, albeit from folks who knew where our political sympathies lay.

Because I was tied up at the seminary with exams and meetings, we agreed that Judith would meet Mr. Yén and Abe for lunch. When she got back to the house that afternoon, she had quite a story to tell. When she arrived at Mr. Yén's apartment, he told her that although the guest had called earlier in the morning saying he would be there for lunch, he hadn't arrived. Judith waited for an hour. Mr. Yén called the man's hotel room and reported to Judith that someone sounding like the police had answered. Mr. Yén hung up, reported to Judith, and she left for home.

Judith was concerned about the failure of the friend to appear, as was Mr. Yén. As she came out of the narrow alley that led to his apartment, she saw that a woman was following her. Instead of taking a taxi right away, she walked down the street, stopping to look in the windows of shops. Whenever she stopped, the woman behind her stopped. She continued down the street for a couple of blocks until she was certain that the woman was in fact following her. She hailed a cab but didn't come directly home. She changed cabs several times before finally coming up the mountain to the seminary.

When she told me what had happened we knew that things had moved into a new phase. Late that night, Mr. Yén showed up at our door in a T-shirt perspiring heavily and as nervous as we had ever seen him. He reported that Abe had been arrested and that he had been taken in for questioning. The police told him that the "gift" he had was a cake containing potassium chlorate, which had multiple common uses in labs but was also a substance from which bombs could be made. He said his suspicions had led him not to give the gift to Judith when she was at his home earlier in the day. Abe had my name and phone number in his pocket. Since Mr. Yén was a member of the National Assembly, he did not think he would be arrested. He did not know about us.

We assured him that we didn't know Abe apart from Mr. Yén's introduction months earlier and that no one had ever suggested that we would receive material for making bombs. I thanked him for not giving the gift to Judith. We said a hasty good-bye and realized that it would probably be the last time we would see Mr. Yén. Whatever was going on, we knew that there would be little delay. We would be arrested and deported, or arrested, tried, and imprisoned.

We collapsed into chairs in the living room and tried to make sense of what was happening.

"The net is closing," Judith said with a nervous laugh.

The adrenaline was pumping and the strain must have shown on both our faces.

"I guess we won't have to wait long now," I replied without asking the question that was really on my mind. What was this was going to mean for Judith's pregnancy? At five months, she had successfully passed the early critical period. But she had been suffering from severe headaches ever since we returned in September. Our family physician had done some tests and decided that the cause was stress. The diagnosis made sense to us because we knew in a way that the doctor couldn't know what pressures we were under. Now I worried that the pressure of an imminent arrest would increase the stress level to a point where both Judith and the pregnancy were further threatened.

We tried to put the things Mr. Yén said together as if they were pieces of a puzzle. Somehow, because we knew that we had no part in a plan to make and use explosives, we thought we had been set up. Our experience with the effectiveness of the people in Japan with Peter's escape convinced us that they would not have been party to such an ill-conceived plan. The only thing that made sense to us was that we had been set up by the KMT to provide undeniable proof of our guilt in a crime for which they could arrest us. Were the two men from Japan KMT agents, or at least hired by them? What was Mr. Yén's role? Not inconceivable to us was the possibility that under pressure from something the government might have had on him that Mr. Yén participated in the trap. We had never been clear about how he met the two Japanese men and why he wanted us to "help entertain" them.

The more we talked about it, the less plausible his knowingly being party to the set up seemed. It didn't square with what we thought we knew about him, so we moved on to assume that he had been unknowingly used to set us up but that he suspected something about the man and his "gift" for us. If he had had the package at his house when Judith was there, as he said he did, he could have placed the smoking gun in our possession.

We talked about what ifs until nothing we thought we knew made complete sense. Emotional exhaustion allowed both of us a few hours of sleep. When morning came, taking care of the kids and getting ready for classes provided momentary distraction from the thought that the police might show up at the door at any time. But they didn't.

Days went by and nothing happened. I had a meeting scheduled in Tainan to continue negotiating the merger of the seminaries. In an air of unreality, I took the train down for the meeting and came back the next day. While there I was able to tell the principal of Tainan Theological College and also a confidant, Dan Beeby, what had happened and that our arrest seemed imminent. Being able to share the uncertainty with good friends was comforting.

The day I arrived back in Taipei, Bud arrived from Hong Kong. I had forgotten that he was coming. Once I told him what had happened, I suggested that he might not want to stay with us. He said that since he was already at the house, he might as well stay the night and return to Hong Kong as planned a few days later. When he came back from a taxi trip to Taipei to do some missionary business at the Methodist office, he said that he had been followed from the seminary.

On Monday, February 22, making sure we weren't followed, we met Tony at a coffee shop on Chung Shan North Road in Taipei. Bud gave him a thousand U.S. dollars that had come from the American Friends Service Committee for families of political prisoners. Tony said that he and Wei would take the train the next day and distribute the money in the south. We told him about the cake incident and said that if the story was true and Abe had my name as the recipient, we would either be arrested and tried or expelled. Tony said he knew nothing of Abe or a plan to use explosives, and he was certain Matthew didn't either. Because they didn't know anything about it, he wasn't worried, he said with his usual confident smile. Tony had been out of prison only eighteen months and Matthew twenty-eight. Judith and I were near tears when the meal ended, not about what was going to happen to us but because we were likely seeing Tony for the last time and that we weren't going to have an opportunity to say good-bye to Matthew. Bud shook hands with Tony. Judith and I hugged him. He sat back down at the table to give us time to leave the restaurant and get a taxi.

"You know," I said to Bud as we sat in the living room after we got home from the restaurant and the kids were in bed, "we've got a trunk full of the articles in the closet of my study."

"Having the government get their hands on those is probably not a good idea," Bud said.

"Should we burn them?" I asked.

"Don't you think whoever is watching the house will see the smoke from the chimney and think something funny is going on?" Bud asked, pointing to the perspiration showing through my shirt on the warm March evening.

"I don't think they'll see the smoke," Judith said. "The outside lights are all below the roof level. I don't think you can even see the chimney from outside when those lights are on."

"Might as well take the chance," Bud said.

"I don't think we have a choice," I said, heading down the two stairs in the narrow hall that led to my study.

I disassembled one of the packets, wadded up the individual sheets of mimeographed paper, and started a fire. It was quickly apparent how big a job this was going to be. It was like burning a steamer trunk full of magazines.

With the project taking so much time, Judith finally went to bed. Soon, the living room was like a furnace. Bud and I took off our shirts and continued to feed the fire. We were soaked with sweat. Near midnight, I put the last of the papers in and Bud went to take a shower. Throughout the evening both of us had expected the police to arrive and interrupt the burning. Were they not outside? Could they have not seen the smoke pouring from the chimney? Since there wasn't a knock at the door, I assumed not.

I walked into the kitchen for a glass of water without turning on the light. I stood by the open window watching the lane that led up to the administration building not twenty-five feet from where I stood. There was a dim light at the corner of the building just across our driveway. My heart almost stopped as the figure of a man materialized out of the darkness. I froze in place. All I could see were the white cuffs and the white of his shirt behind his tie. I wasn't imagining it; he was walking directly toward the kitchen door. At least the papers are burned, I thought. Will they arrest us tonight?

But the man didn't come up to the door. Since he had been right outside, I dared not move. Everyone was now asleep in the house except for me. I don't know how long I waited in the darkness, but I finally decided to go to bed. Sleep did not come. I have never been particularly afraid of the dark, but that night the darkness was terrifying. I pleaded for daylight to come: Take me and arrest me, I thought. Do whatever you want to do with me. Just do it after it is daylight. When the gray of the dawn was visible outside the window, I could feel the tension easing. I went to sleep and didn't wake till mid-morning. The terror of that night would replay itself a thousand times in dreams I would have over the next ten years.

Matthew and Tony wouldn't make the trip south to distribute the funds. On Tuesday, February 23, 1971, five days before 2-28, the police went to their homes and arrested them. The government didn't announce their arrests. We learned about the arrests the next day when a Miss Chen, a friend of Peter, showed up at our door at the seminary and gave us the news. She knew only the fact of their arrests, not why they had been arrested. Because of the Yén affair, we were concerned, but not panicked. Rounding up potential troublemakers before February 28 as a measure to prevent any efforts to observe the massacre was not an uncommon practice, and we had already heard about people being detained in recent weeks. In years past, most were released after the threat to the anniversary had passed. Given the timing, we hoped that would be the case with Matthew and Tony, but we knew such hope was a slender thread. It made more sense that they had been arrested attempting to deliver the money to families. And there wasn't anything we could do to help them.

Three days passed, and they hadn't come for us. Months earlier, we had arranged to meet Selig Harrison, the East Asia Bureau chief for the *Washington Post,* on his visit to Taiwan. Someone told him that we could arrange for him to meet dissident Taiwanese. We had arranged for a dinner with a member of the Provincial Assembly, who had a reputation of being independent and not intimidated by the KMT. We decided to go ahead with the dinner on Saturday night, February 27, but would make sure we were not followed to the restaurant. We met Harrison at his hotel and warned him that we might be followed. As we started down the street, we saw a gray suit tagging along behind us. We crossed and recrossed the street to make sure, and each time he crossed and recrossed behind us.

Thinking we had nothing to lose and perhaps emboldened because of the person we were with, we decided to confront him. When the light changed, instead of going across, we turned around and approached the man who was not five yards behind us.

"You are from what agency?" I asked the surprised man in Mandarin.

"No, no, no," he said, waving his hands and stepping out into the street.

"Why are you following us?" Judith asked in her pure Mandarin, moving toward him while he frantically looked for an opportunity to dash through the wall of cars passing by. "Our friend from the *Washington Post* would be interested in knowing," she shouted after him as he dashed between cars to get away from us. It would not be the last time we would see him.

We hailed a cab, changed a couple of times, and then went on to the restaurant, where we met our Taiwanese friend.   Peter had introduced us to the assemblyman a couple of years before, but we knew him mostly for his reputation as a thorn in the side of the KMT. He answered all of Harrison's questions in Mandarin, which we in turn translated into English. On the question of whether Taiwan should be reunited with the Mainland, he repeated the refrain that we heard so often over the years: "We don't want Mao and we don't want Chiang! Communism or anti-Communism has nothing to do with it. We are Taiwanese, not Chinese, and should be able to govern ourselves."

We were impressed with Harrison's knowledge and sensitivity; so when he asked if he could see us again to get better acquainted, we invited him to dinner at our house on March 2, three days away. He would come to the house on Tuesday, but we would be unable to serve him dinner.

Chapter Nineteen
Arrest and Deportation

Thus hath the candle singed the moth.

— William Shakespeare, *Merchant of Venice (1600)*

We were preparing to sit down to lunch with David Chen, principal of the seminary, when three men in plain clothes and a fourth in a black Foreign Affairs Police uniform came to the door and asked us to accompany them to headquarters to hear some "advice from Colonel Wang, head of that office." We asked them to wait until we finished our lunch, and they agreed, seating themselves in the living room not six feet from the dining room table. We just looked at the food in front of us, engaging in a nervous banter, words to fill the pall that had fallen over the room with the arrival of these uninvited guests. David was Peter's cousin, but as far as we knew, he was never involved in any sort of political activity. He didn't seem rattled by the presence of these officials. We wondered if he had been invited or ordered to be present to witness the arrest.

Elizabeth was at nursery school and our amah had Richard in the kitchen. David said he would see that both would be cared for until we returned. We were taken in an unmarked police car to the main foreign affairs police station, next to City Hall. Upon arrival, we were ushered up two flights of stairs to the third floor, where Colonel Wang and two other men awaited us.

The five of us then went into a large, green-carpeted room. Overstuffed chairs lined three of the walls; coffee tables were placed at intervals in front of the chairs. We sat down in one corner, and Colonel Wang proceeded to read a brief statement in English. In essence it said that we had violated the regulations controlling aliens in the Republic of China and had committed "unfriendly actions against the government of the ROC." Because of this, we were being expelled from the country and must leave within forty-eight hours. During that period our "movements and living" would be severely restricted. Wang then presented me with a single typed copy of the statement and asked me to sign at the bottom, where there was a sentence indicating that I had read the statement and understood it. I said that I would be glad to sign it if I could have a copy. Wang said there was only one copy and if I didn't wish to sign it I didn't have to. I didn't.

The colonel went on to explain that a representative from the Yangmingshan bureau (controlling the district where we lived) would answer any further questions we might have and would be waiting at the house when we returned. I pressed him for an explanation of the term "unfriendly actions," and he replied that he didn't have time to explain it to me. We asked if the American Embassy had been notified of our deportation order. Wang said that it had and that a representative would come to see us that day.

We were driven directly back to our house, accompanied by a man and a woman in plain clothes. Awaiting us at home were another man and woman, also without uniforms. From then on we had the two men and two women in our living room at all times. Several men in gray suits milled around outside the door while jeeps, motorcycles, and men encircled the house. The representative from the Yangminshan bureau never showed up, and any further explanation of the charges or our exact limitations was never given. We soon learned, though, what was meant by "severe restrictions on our movements and living."

As we entered the house, the phone rang. Selig Harrison was on the line. He was calling to ask what time he should arrive for dinner. Judith managed to blurt out to him that we were being deported just before one of the two men in the room—a man as tall as I was and much larger —snatched the phone from her hand and pulled the line out of the wall. We were completely cut off from the outside.

We made several requests to our guards to allow us to ask Bishop Nall in Hong Kong where we should go and to make flight arrangements. The requests were all refused. They anxiously worked to keep word of our deportation from spreading. One of the guards later told us that they feared that our friends might rally and stage a riot on our behalf.

We asked again to see a representative from the embassy. We were assured that they knew about our situation. One of the guards said that had the embassy not consented to our deportation, it wouldn't have been ordered. We wondered about the right of a foreign embassy to approve the deportation of one of its nationals. The guard maintained that he was telling the truth. We would later learn that the embassy knew two days before our arrest.

In the hours that followed, we tried to get organized and pack, but it was hard to concentrate. We wondered if anyone knew what was happening and what the people on campus were thinking about the massive police presence there. Five-year-old Elizabeth seemed unaware that anything special was going on. Since she was allowed to go and come freely from the house, we wrote a brief message to Bob Montgomery, a Presbyterian missionary on campus whose daughter played with Elizabeth. We wrapped the message around a piece of gum, replaced the tinfoil wrapper, and put it back into the paper sleeve and into an opened pack. We told Elizabeth to go directly to the Montgomery's house and give it to one of her friend's parents and to please not offer a stick to one of the guards on her way out. She did what we asked of her. While the campus was abuzz with speculation about what was happening at our house, Elizabeth delivered the first message to the missionary community.

The living/dining room was not large, perhaps only twelve by sixteen feet. When four guards, one of which was quite large, were seated on the sofa and chairs, the only other places to sit were at the table. When the Taiwanese woman who worked for us put dinner on the table, Elizabeth asked why the guards did not eat with us. I suggested that she ask them. I don't know if she did or not, but she certainly provided entertainment for them. They were amazed at her fluency in both Mandarin and Taiwanese and spent a lot of time chatting with her, and she liked the attention.

After supper, sometime after seven or eight o'clock, we heard loud voices outside the house. We recognized Selig Harrison's voice and tried to open the front door and go out, but a policeman blocked us. Judith then ran to the dining room window, opened it, and shouted, "Sig, they won't let us talk to anyone. Please get the word out." He tried to answer, but at that point was shoved down by one of the policemen. One of the guards inside shouted for me to get Judith away from the window. The guards were pretty angry, especially since they had just told Harrison that we weren't at home. After the incident, we received a lecture on cooperation with the police during "difficult times." Shoving Harrison around probably got our story onto the front page of the next day's _Washington Post_.

After the lecture, we went to the bedroom where, thankfully, they didn't follow us. At nearly ten o'clock, we heard another commotion outside. Thinking that Harrison had returned, Judith ran into the study and out into the front yard through the entrance that had escaped the notice of the police. The visitor wasn't Harrison but Dick Bush, a United Methodist missionary colleague. He was arguing loudly with the policeman surrounding him. Judith shouted that we were being deported and asked him to contact the embassy. He shouted back that he would.

Back in the house, I received a more severe lecture about Judith's behavior.

"Your wife is a _lao you-tyao_ [old grease stick]! If you can't control her, we will take you to jail and you will be separated from your children."

"Both of us wish to cooperate," I responded, "but cooperation is a two-way street, and we haven't seen any cooperation with our request to talk with someone from the U.S. Embassy."

The large man spun on his heels and walked out the door. Our little heart–to-heart chat may have made a difference because at almost midnight the consul, Fred Beattie, showed up. I told him that I didn't want U.S. intervention in the case of our deportation—I didn't want to be associated with the country's long history of such intervention in Chinese affairs—but that I did want information about why we were being treated as criminals and held incommunicado. He admitted that the embassy had some "unofficial" information but that he was not at liberty to share it with us. I would learn later that the embassy felt no hesitation in sharing the "unofficial" charges with Bishop Nall and others about our arrest. The consul said we should cooperate in every possible way and leave the country as quietly as possible. What I felt as I talked to him was that he cared not one whit about us. He was representing a State Department closely allied with the Nationalist government, and we were an embarrassment to both of them.

He helped us in two ways. The next day Clyde and Betty Dunn, United Methodist missionaries, were allowed into the house to discuss property and moving matters with us. The guards sat with us to see that we didn't talk about anything except packing and shipping arrangements. He had also arranged for permission for Judith to be taken to see the obstetrician. She was five months pregnant; considering her history and all of this stress, we were concerned that she might lose the baby. She was taken to MacKay Hospital with two guards—a man and a woman—from the four who had been staying in the house. Although he probably wondered about having guards stationed outside the examining room, the doctor's report on Judith and the baby was good.

When Judith the two guards left for her appointment, the other female guard went outside to join those surrounding the house. I made coffee for myself and offered a cup to the remaining guard. He sat down across the table from me.

"I know that you are not criminals," he said. "This is really a political matter. You must realize that we are in difficult times here. The enemy is just across the straits, and our international position is deteriorating at a rapid rate. In another time, I do not think you would be expelled for what you have done, and I think you will probably be able to return to Taiwan before very long."

"Do you really think so?" I asked, recalling what one of the other guards had said about concerns that our arrest might cause riots.

"Oh, yes!"

"You know what really worries me is whether or not your government will give us any problems taking Richard outside the country," I said. "He is now a U.S. citizen, but I know that people of the Han born in Taiwan are considered Chinese citizens no matter what passport they carry."

"What kind of monsters do you think we are?" he asked. "We would never do something like that."

I think he probably believed it. I would not be sure until we had Richard out of the country. It would be this same guard who, against his orders, would allow some of our friends to come to the door on Thursday morning and say good-bye. We made a point of thanking him for this courtesy.

We spent Wednesday evening packing and writing simple instructions for the disposition of our things. The consul visited us once more mainly to tell us that the embassy was unwilling to disclose any of the particulars about why we had been arrested. He told us that we would be leaving on a China Airlines flight to Hong Kong at 1:15 P.M. Thursday. This was the first word about when we would be deported. With things apparently settled, I had no trouble sleeping Wednesday night. Since I did not know that the story was already big news outside Taiwan, I had no idea of the "new world" I would enter on Thursday.

Last-minute packing and getting Richard and Liz ready to go was the agenda for Thursday morning. The Dunns showed up about an hour before we were to leave. Mary Ella Brentlinger, another Methodist missionary, managed to get into the house with the Dunns and actually got away with it for a while before the guards realized she didn't belong and ordered her out.

We left the house by car at noon, greatly encouraged by the presence of several friends keeping a vigil of sorts outside the circle of police around the house. When we passed the administration building, many students and faculty members were gathered on both sides of the road to say good-bye. Of course, they made no gestures to wave; they just watched. Their presence there put each of them at considerable risk. I knew I could not wave to them. In an already emotionally charged atmosphere, I began to cry. There were cars of secret police both in front of and behind us.

Overcome with emotion at the bravery of so many students and faculty daring to stand and watch as we left, I was slow to sense the magnitude of the police operation to get us to the airport. Holding Richard on my lap, I looked across at Elizabeth, her face glued to the other window of the black limousine taking us down the mountain. What I saw out her window as we descended the mountain, passed the Generalissimo's home in Shih-lin, and moved into Taipei were gray suits stationed on both sides of the road at regular intervals. Rowland Van Es, who had gotten word in Tainan and come by train to witness our departure, followed our motorcade down the mountain. Soldiers, he said, were posted every ten or twenty yards along the five miles to Songshan Airport.[25]

"What the hell are they afraid of—us?" I asked.

"If so, they are crazier than we thought," Judith replied as she watched the unnumbered sentries flash past.

As we traveled down Minchuan Road to the entrance, the distance between the sentries diminished, and as we entered the circle in front of the airport the gray suits were shoulder to shoulder around the entire perimeter.

Our car drove directly to the entrance to the VIP lounge. Inside were more men and women, some soldiers and some gray suits. The large room was so full of them

---

[25] Rowland Van Es, "Repressed Memories: Soldiers Standing Every 10-20 Yards on the Route to the Airport," in Lindai Gail Arrigo and Lynn Miles, *A Borrowed Voice: Taiwan Human Rights Through International Networks, 1960-1980* (Hanyao Color Printing Co: Taipei, Taiwan, 2008) p. 197.

that it was almost like a Lantern Festival crowd, except they were all security personnel.

I recognized one of them as the man we had confronted when he was following us with Selig Harrison a week earlier. I addressed him in Chinese. "So we meet again," I said. He responded with a smile, "Now we are old friends." It took half an hour for four people to go through our few bags. They went through everything—jars of cold cream, tubes of toothpaste, and every piece of paper in my briefcase.

A difficulty arose when they found some sermons I had in my briefcase. Since they were written in Romanized Chinese, no one there could read them. They assumed they were some kind of secret code. So I spent several minutes with one of the men, reading the sermons to him and a couple of others who were looking on. I pointed to the words as I read. Finally, they decided that they were what I said they were and allowed me to put them back into my briefcase. I felt a certain irony as I preached to one of my guards in my last moments in Taiwan.

Another difficulty arose when they tried to listen to some of our tape recordings and stumbled onto some Atayal hymns we had recorded. No one there understood the words of that aboriginal language (not a Chinese dialect but a part of the Malay-Polynesian language family).

They might have taken more time on the tapes and sermons, but they had already held up this flight well beyond its scheduled departure. Everyone was on the plane but us. The American consul, Mr. Beattie, showed up at the last minute. We couldn't help informing him that he always managed to show up when he was no longer useful.

We were driven from the terminal to the boarding ramp of the airplane. Only then did we get the first hint of the publicity our departure was receiving. The ramp was surrounded by reporters filming and taking pictures of us. While the mood in the VIP lounge had been quiet and subdued, here we were confronted by a crowd of reporters on both sides of the runway shouting out questions and a sea of flashbulbs going off in our faces.

I had Richard on my back and Judith had Elizabeth by the hand. Unnerved by the noise and lights, Elizabeth froze in front of the steps. In a genuine gesture to help, one of the policemen accompanying us onto the plane scooped her up and carried her up the steps. Already frightened and now being seemingly separated from us, Elizabeth began to kick and scream. A film crew from NBC brought in to cover our departure caught it all. The first our parents in Texas and Massachusetts knew of our arrest was when they saw that film clip on television.

Having already seen all of the reporters at the airport in Taipei, we weren't very surprised by the mob of reporters that met our plane in Hong Kong. Bishop Nall, accompanied by missionaries from Hong Kong and Chinese pastors, pushed through the crowd promising that we would speak to the press the next day.

We were put up in a family suite at the YMCA on Waterloo Road. Selig Harrison followed us to Hong Kong and found us there. Since we had never held a press conference before, once Richard and Elizabeth were down for the night, Harrison spent several hours in our room advising us about how to conduct ourselves at the next day's event. We let him know that we would not say anything to further jeopardize the Taiwanese or our colleagues.

Harrison's most important admonition was not to end any sentence without including whatever qualifications we needed to make. So when they asked us about our relationships with dissident Taiwanese, we were to be careful to say that we were friends with both dissidents *and persons who were supporters of the government*, which was certainly true. When asked if we were linked to the Taiwanese Movement for Independence, we would say that while we knew many who were unhappy with the government and wanted to see an independent Taiwan, *were unaware of any organized effort in Taiwan,* which was also true. When reporters asked why we were arrested, we could quite honestly say that we didn't know beyond "actions unfriendly to the government of the Republic of China." We could also say that in Taiwan, having contact with people who disagreed with government policy was construed as "unfriendly actions," which was true.

What we could have said but didn't was that the government might have arrested us because of our involvement with Peter and his escape, but we were pretty sure that they didn't know it. We might have said that we were engaged in aiding families of political prisoners, but we didn't know if they knew that, either. We were not about to make things more difficult for Matthew and Tony. We knew that the government knew about the Japanese visitor with the gift, but we assumed that was a KMT setup. Harrison had heard from the American ambassador that we were importing explosives, but he didn't believe him. We simply told him we weren't. He said not to mention it unless asked directly. It wasn't and we didn't.

I don't know why Harrison took the time to help us. Certainly he had access to us that no other reporters had, but he didn't use any of the material we discussed that night in our room. We were deeply grateful for his counsel.

During the next two days, we held a press conference, had a series of interviews with journalists, and talked with our area secretary, Ed Fisher, by phone in New York. Ed had learned of our arrest and deportation from the *New York Times*. Within days of our arrival in Hong Kong, Bishop Nall and his wife returned to Taiwan. The bishop was anxious to see what havoc our expulsion had created among the Methodist faithful. The Nalls graciously allowed us to stay in their rented house on a mountain on Hong Kong Island overlooking the harbor and Kowloon. We had a few days to rest while the bishop and our area secretary decided what to do with us.

On March 9 we wrote a lengthy letter to our colleagues in Taiwan, which included the details of our house arrest

and the charges we were hearing that the KMT was
unofficially releasing:

Dear Friends,

*We do not know what our expulsion will mean for
you in Taiwan—whether it marks the beginning of a
new level of pressure on the church or whether ours is
a special case. Either way, you have the right to ask
us what grounds the government had for expelling us.
The government in Taiwan has chosen so far not to
make any formal charges, but it has released several
suggestions through "unofficial government sources."*

*We would like to begin by making two negative
statements: (1) We have never been in contact with or
in the employ of any agency of the United States
government. A local Hong Kong pro-Nationalist
newspaper (Kuai Pao) charged in an editorial that we
were agents of the CIA and were forcing Nixon's two-
China policy on Taiwan. (2) We have not participated
in any acts of violence nor have we been party to any
conspiracy to use violence. Again, through "unofficial
government sources" this charge has been made.*

*Having said this, we want to make clear to you that
we have done things that the government in Taiwan
would consider "unfriendly," the term that they used
to us. We did not restrict our friendships to those
people who supported the government or to those who
were apolitical. Most of our friends would fall in those
two categories, but we also had friends who were in
various ways opposed to the government. The Chinese
newspapers in Hong Kong all played up our supposed
relation to the independence movement. At the press
conference the question was put to us directly. Our
response was that as far as we know, there is no
independence movement as such existing in Taiwan.
We believe there are probably many small, unrelated
groups in Taiwan, often with quite differing views
about what the island's future should be and how it
should be achieved. They are united only in the fact*

that all are opposed to the present government of Taiwan. That some of our friends were related to such groups is quite possible, although we never had any direct contact with or knowledge of such groups. Having friends who were regarded as anti-government, however, would certainly be considered an unfriendly act by the Nationalist government.

From the time we first arrived on Taiwan we felt that any ministry we had to its people demanded such wide contacts as we made. We are proud of our friends there, whatever their political positions. We tried neither to censor them for their views nor to lead them into other ideas. Most of you were, of course, well aware of our feelings about these contacts. We felt that we had to act as we did, and are willing to accept the consequences of our acts, even if these included false charges. We do regret, however, any pressure you who are still in Taiwan may receive as a result of our actions. We can only hope that such pressure will not materialize. But we are living in a period of great uncertainty in regard to Taiwan and its international relationships. Because the American government is so deeply involved in all that affects Taiwan, it is very likely that Americans living there will increasingly find themselves under pressures of one kind or another. Please know that our prayers and thoughts will be with all of you; we wish we could be with you in body as well as in spirit.

Closing,
Judith and Milo

We didn't say anything in the letter that wasn't true, but there was much that we didn't say. Our first priority in talking about our arrest and deportation was not to make the situation of our Taiwanese friends any more difficult than it already was. Since the moment we had agreed to be politically active five years before, we often discussed with our Taiwanese associates the likelihood of a day when they would be made to suffer in ways far more severe than we would. Although we wouldn't know the details for over a year, on February 23 that day had arrived for Hsieh and Wei.

Chapter Twenty
Some Not Fireproof

The Inquisitor manages every thing;
caprice regulates much, hope corrupts them,
so that in the straits in which they are placed,
there is but little room left for truth.

—Cicero (1st Century B.C.)

Hsieh T'sung-min, who we called "Tony," was arrested on Tuesday, February 23, 1971. It was the day after Bud, Judith, and I met him in a coffee shop across the street from MacKay Hospital, where Bud passed a thousand dollars in U.S. currency to him for the families of political prisoners. Wei T'ing-chao, who we called "Matthew," was arrested the same day. Like thousands before them, there was no announcement of the arrest, and there wouldn't be for months. No charges were filed, and they wouldn't be until a year, later when they were tried in a secret military court.

Torture, a calculated assault on a prisoner's mind, body, and dignity, was routine for extracting confessions. "We have eighteen techniques," an agent boasted to Tony. "I want information—true and false."

Tony was not allowed sleep on the night of his arrest or on any of the following eight nights. Instead, he was hung in midair and handcuffed with one arm stretched over his shoulder. In a letter he wrote after he was able to slip out of prison months later, he described those first weeks:

They attacked me and kept me sleepless from February 23 to March 2, and from March 8 to March 13. Hysterically they screamed and howled... They handcuffed my hands on my back, knocked at my ears, kicked my stomach, blow my legs and beat my ribs fiercely. A jet of brown vomit flowed from my mouth. I felt a piercing pain in my chest, and was unable to walk for a week.

The inquisitor's first questions were about Peng's escape. How had Hsieh communicated with Ambassador McConnaughy for the American government to get Peng out of the country? They said they knew Peng had left on a U.S. military plane from the Ching Chuan Kang (CCK) Air Base near Taichung, which was used by the United States Air Force to support the war in Southeast Asia. They said they also knew that Peng had stopped in Japan and met with Yasuhiro Nakasone, head of the Agency of Defense.

Not only had Tony never had any contact with anyone from the U.S. Embassy, he didn't know how Peng had gotten out of the country. In planning Peng's escape, we had decided that we couldn't involve Matthew or Tony. The risk to them was too great if the plan failed. The fact that it was successful didn't remove them from suspicion. What his inquisitors didn't ask him about was my and Judith's involvement in the escape. Apparently, we were not suspects.

Since the story he made up about Peng's escape didn't make sense, the inquisitors moved to the bombing of the USIS in Tainan the previous October and the more recent the bombing of Bank of America in Taipei on February 5. They told him to write down a story of how both incidents happened. He made up a story and gave it to them. The next day they came back, saying that they had given it to Chiang Ching-kuo, and he said that Hsieh hadn't committed either offense.

The questions, asked during intermittent torture, were now about my and Judith's involvement with him. They told Tony they knew all about Abe and the attempt to bring in potassium chlorate inside the Japanese cake. They said knew that the cake was to be delivered to me and then passed on to someone else. Hsieh said over and over that he didn't know anything about explosive-making material to be delivered to him. All he knew was what we and Mr. Yén had told him that after Abe had been arrested. Tony had not been asked to receive and make explosives and neither had we.

The inquisitors quickly abandoned the Abe affair and turned to the bombing of Bank of America three weeks earlier. They said that it was probably done by an American businessman because many of them did business with that bank, and they suspected me. Tony said that I wasn't a businessman but a teacher and never left the seminary. He said that Judith was pregnant and wouldn't be able to plant a bomb. They insisted that Tony write another story— this one involving us. On the day or two before we were arrested on March 2, he wrote one that had Judith placing the bomb in the bank. For that he was rewarded with a week without torture.

On March 8, the inquisitors returned and said that his story about us was false. No one at the bank had ever seen the pictures they showed them of Judith. They would have remembered a pregnant woman, they said. The torture began again and continued without interruption until mid-March. On March 15, a local Chinese newspaper ran an ad taken out by Tony's sister. In large type, like a headline, it said that Hsieh had been arrested on February 23 because of his relationship with Peng. Tony's sister had been present when the police came to get him. When they searched his room, Tony feared they would discover the thousand dollars, so he turned it over to them with his other personal possessions. The arresting officers refused to give her a receipt. In the ad she demanded a receipt for the thousand dollars. According to Don Shapiro, a stringer for the _New York Times_ who visited the sister after seeing the ad, her protest embarrassed authorities. They had been caught off guard by the ad—a news item would have been caught by the censors—and after no small resistence gave her a receipt. They warned her to keep quiet. One of them told her that the money had come from "Reverend Thornberry."

From our safe haven in Hong Kong, we were unaware of what was happening to Tony and Matthew and the ripples our arrest and deportation were causing in relations between Taiwan and the U.S. Years later, when some State Department materials were declassified, the picture became clearer.

In a memo preparing the head of the U.S. State Department's East Asia section for a visit from GRC Ambassador Chow in Washington on March 4, Director, Office of Republic of China Affairs, Thomas P. Shoesmith said that the GRC "claimed to have evidence, including tapes of conversations Thornberry allegedly has had with Taiwanese over the past year, that Thornberry had been actively encouraging Taiwanese to engage in violent action against the government and other subversive activities. In one taped conversation Thornberry allegedly offered to assist in obtaining explosives."

Shoesmith said that they had checked with some Foreign Service offices that knew us and everyone agreed that we were "actively engaged in encouraging and supporting Taiwan independence activities, although their remarks do not suggest they believe the Thornberrys would have gone as far as GRC evidence suggests." Such evidence was not shared with the U.S.

The problem, Green said, was that the stories in the *Washington Post* and *New York Times* were portraying the story "as an expression of GRC dissatisfaction with the U.S.'s China policy..." Although the U.S. was urging the GRC to clarify the basis of its actions in arresting us, the only response was that "we did not conform to the laws prescribed for the conduct of foreigners residing in China." If the GRC refused to release more specific charges, Green said, the incident "would evoke strong adverse public and Congressional criticism of the GRC."

In a memo on March 9, Shoesmith reported on the meeting with Ambassador Chow. Chow had threatened "serious consequences," suggesting anti-American demonstrations or actions against American personnel and property in response to any other "subversive activities" by Americans. Our case, lamented Shoesmith, could "seriously damage relations at a particularly inopportune time." He worried that there would be other incidents: "There is no shortage of American graduate students, missionaries et al. with both ardent views on Taiwanese independence and a willingness to conduct themselves as if they were fireproof moths." Shoesmith concluded that the U.S. was in for "a period of general stiffening of our relations with the GRC."

To contain Congressional criticism, Green suggested that the unofficial charges be shared with representatives and senators. He also said that the nature of the charges should be "disclosed to his parent organization, the United Methodist Church."

On March 11, while we were staying in their house in Hong Kong, Bishop Nall met with his old friend Ambassador McConnaughy in Taipei. The Ambassador emphasized that the information he was providing was on a "very confidential basis and not for publication." He also said that the U.S. State Department was in no position to evaluate the evidence, which they had not seen, and thus could not pass judgment on the charges. This caveat notwithstanding, the American ambassador said that the GRC claimed to have "incontrovertible evidence" of sedition and violence against the GRC. He said that I had been "in secret contact with Peng Ming-min both before and after his escape and had served as a channel for clandestine messages between Peng and his friends and relatives on Taiwan." This charge was true. What the absence of any reference to my role Peng's escape suggested was that neither the GRC nor the U.S. suspected such involvement.

McConnaughy mentioned the cake incident, saying that I "apparently was involved in some way in an effort by Abe to bring potassium chlorate into Taiwan" and that Abe had confessed that he was "bringing the potassium chlorate and letter to Thornberry."

Then, the ambassador said that the GRC had told him that they had taped conversations in which I made incriminating statements about how I spent four hours a day with Taiwanese students urging them to overthrow the GRC, how I advocated sabotage against military and police vehicles, and how on January 16 I told "listeners that the situation was favorable for an uprising" and that if dynamite was needed from abroad, I could get it. Of course, neither Ambassador McConnaughy nor any U.S. personnel were allowed to hear any tapes.

McConnaughy closed by saying that "the evidence was sufficient to bring Thornberry to trial on charges carrying a severe penalty," but the decision not to do so was taken out of regard for U.S.-GRC relations.

Although we were staying in the Nalls' house in Hong Kong while this interview took place, I would not have an opportunity to discuss the charges with Bishop Nall. We were called back to the U.S. before the Nalls returned to Hong Kong. The bishop believed the charges and passed them on to the board of missions as the truth, not with even the caveats that the American ambassador had made. I have been and will be forever grateful that our area secretary, Edwin Fisher, and the leadership of the General Board of Global Ministries chose to believe us and not Bishop Nall.

Ed Fisher was ready to appoint us for work in another part of East Asia. He considered not bringing us back to the U.S. but simply assigning us somewhere else in the area. Chung Chi College in Hong Kong invited me to teach there. Unfortunately, before the Hong Kong government could act on our request for visas, they informed the board that the U.S. State Department had requested that Hong Kong not grant us visas. The board had little choice but to bring us back to the United States.

Almost thirteen months after they had been arrested, Hsieh and Wei were secretly tried and sentenced, Hsieh to fifteen years and Wei to twelve. In prison, as Hsieh put it, there were "two societies": the formal administration and the prisoners' underground. Prisoners who distributed food and cleaned the prison cells provided some of the opportunities for communication with other prisoners. Hsieh arranged for the working prisoners to sweep up small notes from the floor and deposit them in other cells. Floor sweepings were returned to their cells with information on the cases of other prisoners. Hsieh and Wei not only gathered information about hundreds of their fellow prisoners' families, they also managed to get the lists out to us to send to Amnesty International. Through that underground, the information they were able to gather was not only from the political prison they were in but also often from other prisons around the island.

Now confined under greater security than before, Hsieh still tried to get the word out about what was happening to him and others. Months went by and he couldn't find a way to get a message out. The prisoner in the next cell was a Japanese citizen named Kobayashi, who had written a book about Taiwanese independence and made the mistake of visiting the island. The man was imprisoned for about four months. When he was released and sent back to Japan, he carried a letter from Hsieh in English on shreds of thin paper hidden in his clothing.

On March 29, 1972, an anonymous "friend" in Japan sent a copy of the letter to me with a cover letter addressed to the "Editor." The friend had typed the letter but had also sent a copy of Hsieh's hand-written original. A hand-written note scribbled in red ink on a torn piece of paper said that the original letter would be sent later. I never received the original, but from the copy I could see that the handwriting looked like Hsieh's, and the content left no doubt in my mind that he had written it. It confirmed my fears about the horrors that Hsieh and Wei had been enduring in the thirteen months since their arrests. But the letter also confirmed that at least Hsieh was still alive.

Unable to be reappointed outside the country, I was granted study leave to complete my dissertation. The letter came to me while I was collecting data at the Missionary Research Library at the Union Theological Seminary in New York. I shared the letter with Eleanor Kahn, who was doing research at the library at the same time. Judith and I had introduced her and her husband E. J. to Hsieh when they came to Taiwan a couple of years earlier. E. J., a long-time writer for *The New Yorker*, asked only if I could vouch for the authenticity of the letter. On April 24, the letter was published as an op-ed piece in the *New York Times*. He described his torture in the first weeks and the cases of others in the prison. He concluded his letter with these words:

We are confined separately in solitaire. A sound proof room with a close circuit television transmitter. There is no window or picture in the room. We are not permitted to "walk about" under the sunshine. We are unable to do anything without being watched by some guards. We are taken as a real active hostile threat to the KMT. I consider it is my moral duty to take the matter to you and let it not be buried in the dark room as the other cases were. At least it will bring me peace of mind.

The response in Taiwan was immediate. Although his captors said they wanted to kill him because of the bad publicity his letter generated, the torture stopped until the next time he tried to get a letter out. This one he got as far as the U.S. Navy Post at the American Navy Medical Study Center behind the hospital at Taiwan University. U.S. Naval Security intercepted Hsieh's letter and saw that it was from a political prisoner. They turned the letter over to General Lo, Chief of the General Staff of the GRC, who ordered that the Hsieh be forced to reveal how he got the letter out. Hsieh got so sick from the torture that he had to be hospitalized. Amnesty International sent a doctor into the country to see Hsieh, but the doctor was not allowed to examine him. The doctor's presence, however, seemed to be sufficient for the authorities to put Hsieh in the Taiwan University Hospital, where he was treated and then returned to prison. Years later, in his paper on the White Terror, Hsieh told this story to remind his readers "that the U.S. Navy not only patrolled the Taiwan Straight for Taiwanese security, but also defended Chiang Kai-shek's martial law rule."

Our youngest daughter, Katy, was born two months after we returned to the States. Her Chinese name was "Mei Sheng" (born in America). In our first year back, we met with Taiwanese groups wherever we traveled, wrote articles about Taiwan, and spoke wherever invited, including a Taiwanese rally in front of the Lincoln Memorial in Washington, D.C. on April 1, 1972. Increasingly, however, we needed to find lives that weren't based in Taiwan, a place we never expected to see again.

There was another reason why we pulled back from our Taiwan activities. When the board of missions tried to appoint us to teach at the Union Theological Seminary in the Philippines and learned that the government there would not give us a visa because our State Department had asked them not to allow us into the country, our sense that we had been blacklisted by our government was confirmed. We learned that the FBI was questioning all of my former students who had come to America to study. They asked the students if I was prone to violence, if I was a "bomb thrower." I concluded that I was a liability not only to friends in Taiwan but also to the Taiwanese in the United States.

While I was finding another life, Hsieh and Wei remained in prison. On September 25, 1975, several months after the death of Chiang Kai-shek, Hsieh and Wei's sentences were reduced to eight years and six months. They were released in 1976. Hsieh left Taiwan and sought sanctuary in the United States. Even there he wasn't safe. His home in California was bombed and burned on separate occasions. The FBI, he said, suspected the KMT. Only in 1987, when martial law was lifted in Taiwan, did Hsieh return to Taiwan. Although forever scarred by his torture in prison, as a Congressman and private citizen Hsieh has worked tirelessly for reparations for political prisoners.

Wei, about whose experience in prison I know almost nothing, was also released in 1976. He married a high school teacher, Chang Ching-hui, the next year and they started a family. Wei was an editor of *Formosa Magazine* when the magazine called for a demonstration in Kaohsiung on Human Rights Day, December 10, 1979. The nonviolent demonstration gave the government an excuse to arrest the leaders. Wei was arrested three days later and imprisoned for another seven and a half years.

Chang Ching-hui and their two children were again without a husband and father. The principal of the high school where she taught protected her from the usual kind of harassment families of political prisoners faced, conditions that Wei spent much of his life chronicling from prison. He was released in 1987 and immediately became active in the still illegal Democratic Progressive Party (DPP). He was also elected to head the Taiwan Political Prisoners Association. As a DPP candidate, Chiang Ching-hui was elected to the National Assembly in 1991. In 1997 Wei published *Taiwan Human Rights Report, 1949-1996.*

In the fall of 1990, I applied for the renewal of my passport, which had expired sometime in the seventies. Not being able to take another assignment overseas, I hadn't bothered trying to renew it. When I planned a trip with Katy and Liz to spend Christmas with Richard in London, it didn't occur to me that there might be a problem. It had, after all, been nineteen years since my arrest and deportation. Weeks went by after I should have received the new passport. After repeated calls to the agency I finally spoke to someone, who told me my request was denied.

Donald Stewart, a former U.S. senator from Alabama who served on the advisory board for the Mission Resource Center at Emory University, where I was the director, enlisted the support of senators Howell Heflin of Alabama and Wyche Fowler and Sam Nunn of Georgia. The next day, an aide from Fowler's office called me and asked, "What did you *do* in Taiwan?" Her tone was not reprimanding but incredulous. "There are so many 'top secret' flags on your file that I'm not sure the senator can help you." I thought that was the end of the matter, but Stewart didn't give up. Apparently, the combined efforts of the three senators made a difference. Sam Nunn's heading the Senate Committee on Armed Services and the Permanent Subcommittee on Investigations probably didn't hurt their efforts.

No one else contacted me, so I had already given up on getting the passport. On the day Katy and Liz were to leave for London without me, a black limo pulled up in front of my house in Atlanta. True to the stereotype, two men in trench coats, hats, and dark glasses knocked at my door. One flashed some kind of government ID—I know, I should have looked more closely, but I didn't—and asked to see my driver's license. I fumbled at getting the laminated document out of my billfold because it was stuck to the plastic window. His impatience was palpable. "Let me just see the billfold," he said. He showed it to his colleague and handed me a brown manila envelope. Saying nothing more, the two men turned around and left. Inside the package was a new passport, good for ten years. I packed my bags and made the evening flight with Katy and Liz.

I passed through Heathrow customs without incident. Maybe Taiwan was behind me now, I thought.

Chapter Twenty-One
The Best Christmas Gift

*You were my father's friend. I have heard about
you from the time I was born.*

— Wei Hsin-ch'i (2003)

"Someone named Michael Fonte who said he knew you
in Taiwan called while you were in the meeting upstairs,"
Jeni Earls called after me as I ran through the office on my
way to the hospital to be with a church member before
surgery. "He said he would contact you at home," I heard
her shout as the door closed behind me. It was September
25, 2003, some thirty-two years after we had been
deported.

On the way to the hospital, I remembered. Michael was
a Roman Catholic Maryknoll missionary in Taiwan while I
was there. We had only been acquaintances in the sixties. I
knew little more than that (at the time) his political
sympathies had been similar to mine. When I got home, I
read an e-mail inviting me to return to Taiwan to be
recognized for my human rights activities three decades
earlier. Other foreigners who had been blacklisted by the
KMT for their human rights activities were also invited.

Sixty-nine days later, I was on my way to the "home"
that in my wildest imaginations I had never expected to see
again. Judith and her husband Jerry were also en route,
as indeed were Liz, Katy, and Richard. As the plane made
its descent into Taiwan Taoyuan International Airport, I
thought back to the day I left thirty-two years earlier. How
and by whom would I be received? I knew Michael Fonte
would be there (but I couldn't imagine who else), and I
wouldn't be left to my own devices.

Michael's was the first familiar face I saw as I cleared
customs. He looked older than I remembered. How many
times would I say that over the next week, and how many

would think the same thing when they saw me? I heard my name called and turned to the mass of people around me. I didn't see the face, but when I heard his laugh I knew it could only be Hsieh Tsung-min. We embraced and re-embraced so many times and so hard that I thought we might crack each others' ribs.

"Come quickly!" he said, "There are others here to meet you."

When we exchanged cards, I saw that Hsieh was the national policy advisor to the president. Hsieh drove to another terminal and waved to a young man standing inside. "This is Mr. Wei's son," Hsieh said as we got out of the car. I had no idea that I would see any of Wei's family. Only in recent days had I learned that I would not be seeing Matthew. On December 28, 1999, during his usual early morning jog on the playground at Hsing-kuo elementary school in Chung-li, Wei T'ing-chao's great heart stopped beating.

Round faced with gold-rimmed glasses and broad shoulders, he looked like his father. We had never seen each other, and he didn't know my English name, but when Hsieh said, "This is T'ang P'ei-Li," Wei's eyes lit up.

"You were my father's friend," were the first words out of his mouth. "I have heard about you from the time I was born."

I told him how sorry I was to learn of his father's death and that he was one of the bravest men I had ever known. A dam of emotion broke and in a torrent of tears, I began to tell him of the times when his father came to the house, played with Liz and Richard, and helped me with my lectures.

Hsieh told me that Wei's widow, Chang Ching-hui, was back in the arrival area, where she was meeting the flight carrying Judith, Jerry, and Liz. Through the large windows, I could see her escorting them past the customs desks and then to where we were waiting. Standing beside her son, she looked tall. I could not see any identification badge, but she was obviously had some authority in the airport. Hsieh later explained that she was chair of the Board of the Taoyuan International Airport Services.

Although it was late and there were no passengers around, our hosts didn't rush to get us on our way to the hotel. It was a moment to be savored. Ching-hui arranged for an airport staff member to collect our cameras and take group pictures. I didn't know when or if I would see Wei's family again, and there was so much I wanted to know about what had happened to Matthew.

"Wei was in prison for much of the time that you were married and when your children were growing up," I said as an opening, inviting Ching-hui to respond.

"The children and I are very proud of Wei," she said. "If there is such a thing as reincarnation," she smiled, "I will gladly marry him again."

Hsieh delivered me to the Ambassador Hotel and reminded me that I would meet Dr. Peng Ming-min at lunch the next day. Peter hosted a lunch for Judith, our families, and colleagues I had not seen for thirty years— Don Wilson, Dick Kagan, and Wendell Karsen. As soon as I shook hands with Dick, he reached into his coat pocket and handed me some folded paper.

"I thought you might like to see this," he said.

I opened it and saw that it was a recently declassified verbatim account of the Nixon and Kissinger meeting with Chou En-lai in 1972.

Since "lunch" was a twenty-five course Taiwanese banquet and I was seated next to Peng, there was time to talk. I had been a little nervous about meeting Peng again after all of these years. He insisted that we sit together, and as it must be with old friends, no matter how long the physical separation, the warmth of the friendship we enjoyed years before seemed to pick up where we had left it. When we addressed him as Dr. Peng, he asked that we call him Peter, the name we had given him when it was not wise to refer to him by his real name. Hsieh sat on the other side of me. The three of us talked with ease.

That evening we attended a banquet hosted by the Taiwan Foundation for Democracy, a nonprofit organization established in 2003 during the exhilarating first months of democracy. The TFD was dedicated to the promotion of democracy and human rights in Taiwan and abroad, the first foundation of its kind in Asia. What we had been told would be a small party was a Taiwanese version of a surprise party, an awards dinner with over two hundred in attendance, including the heads of Foreign Affairs, National Defense, and the Legislature, as well as members of the Democratic Progressive Party.

The thirty of us foreign guests were presented with plaques recognizing our contributions to the struggle for human rights in Taiwan. The presenters were men and women who had been political prisoners during the White Terror. After the name of a foreign honoree was announced, the name of the presenting former prisoner, along with the years he or she served in prison, was announced. The two then approached the stage for the presentation. Some of the former prisoners still looked gaunt, though all of them had been released from prison by 1988 or 1989, when martial law ended. A number of these came to our table to greet us personally. One old man showed me needle marks in the tops of his hands where, during the torture sessions, he had been injected with a substance he still couldn't identify. Each announcement —"[Name] who was in prison for [number of years]"—was like the tolling of a bell for the real heroes in the movement to bring democracy to Taiwan. Peter made the presentations to Judith and me.

On December 8 we had a meeting with another former political prisoner; this one was the first democratically elected president in the history of Taiwan. Chen Shui-bian had been imprisoned in 1985 for pro-democracy writings. While out on bail, he ran for magistrate in Tainan. He lost as most non-KMT candidates still did. After a post-election rally to thank his supporters, Chen's wife, Wu Shu-chen, was run over twice by a truck and permanently paralyzed from the waist down. The KMT said that it was an accident, but most Taiwanese believed that it was an attempt to intimidate Chen. If that was what it was, it didn't work. Chen lost his appeal and went back to prison, but even though paralyzed, his wife ran and was elected to the Legislative Yuan. After the end of martial law, Chen was elected to the Legislative Yuan and later elected mayor of

Taipei. In 2000 he was the DPP candidate for president, and because of a split in the KMT, 39 percent of the vote was enough for Chen to win the election. Although Chen was a democratically elected president, the KMT did not relinquish control of the legislature, the judiciary, or the huge bureaucracies.

Peter, who had returned from exile to Taiwan in 1991 and run unsuccessfully for president in 1996, was Chen's senior advisor. Peter received Judith and me in his office before we went to meet President Chen and took us to a large parlor, where the rest of our group had gathered along with eight television crews. Judith and I started to take seats with our children in seats arranged in a semicircle, but we were directed to seats facing our group at the front. The president spoke about Taiwan's road to democracy and freedom. He spoke interspersing Mandarin with Taiwanese, a practice we had noted in others. One of the Taiwanese members of our group, who had also been in exile, said that he saw the practice as linguistic evidence of an evolving Taiwanese cultural identity without the constraints of the one imposed by the Mainlander-dominated KMT.

President Chen thanked our group for the contributions we had made. Then, speaking directly to our three children and two others who had accompanied their parents, he said, "What your parents did for human rights in Taiwan took time away from you and changed your lives, and so I thank you for your sacrifice as well as theirs."

I realized that the remarks were scripted and what any good politician who had been well briefed on his audience might say, but I was deeply moved. Few children have the opportunity to be thanked by the president of a country for what their parents contributed to human rights.

As we started to leave, President Chen stopped me, took my hand and said, "I'm sorry for what your efforts on our behalf cost you in your own country." We bowed and I went out the door, after which we were led back to Peter's office. Peter said that he had not told Chen about my being blacklisted in the United States and didn't know how he knew.

Exhausted but exhilarated and grateful beyond words, I opened the door to my room at the Ambassador. At the window, the face of the balloon Santa outside stared at me. You old rascal! I thought. What I received this evening was the best Christmas gift ever!

I turned out the lamp beside the bed and pulled up the covers. The only light was from the street as it highlighted the Santa bouncing in the wind. Then I saw it again—the downturn at the corner of the mouth, probably caused by a slip of the artist's brush, but that turned the kindly smile into a sneer. Instead of comfort, I felt like the face was mocking me. I wondered if it was an omen, if the wonder of these days would be sobered by a reality as yet unseen. You're only a damn balloon! I thought as I turned away from the window and went to sleep.

Chapter Twenty-Two
Surprises Still

'Tis strange, but true; for truth is always strange;
Stranger than fiction: if it could be told,
How much would novels gain by the exchange!
How differently the world would men behold!

—Lord Byron's *Don Juan (1823)*

Nothing can take away the joy of those days near Christmas in 2003, but there have been events in the intervening years that have taken me back to the expression on the face in the window. In 2008 President Chen finished his second term and Ma Ying-jeou, the KMT's candidate, won the election.

I was bewildered by how that could happen to the newest and most vibrant democracy in Asia. Charges of corruption made against former President Chen and, some said, a weaker DPP candidate, allowed the KMT to win. I could hardly believe what I read in the news, but, of course, the KMT was and is one of the wealthiest political parties not just in Taiwan but in the world. It never relinquished control of most of the government while a non-KMT President was in office, and the party controlled much of the electronic and print media on the island. While I was there in 2003, a young KMT official said in response to my presentation, "We are not the same KMT we were when you were here." "I hope not," I said. But can a leopard change its spots? I wondered as I walked away.

Invited back to Taiwan in the fall of 2008 to participate in a conference honoring Peng, Hsieh, and Wei on the forty-fourth anniversary of their arrests in 1964—an event many cite as the beginning of the democratization movement in Taiwan—I was asked to speak about my association with the three men. The conference was held in the old Jingmei Military Detention Center, a political prison south of Taipei that was turned into the Taiwan Human Rights Memorial Park in 2007. A Taiwanese student took me on a tour of the prison and explained how it was until martial law ended in 1989. He pointed to the roof where the clothes were routinely hung on a barbed wire fence to dry, making it clearly visible from inside and outside. The pants and shirts were hung upside down as "a signal from those working in the laundry," my guide explained, "that a prisoner had been executed." Clothes were often hung upside down, the young man said.

A water fountain and flowers in the stark center of the prison created an image of hope, but the news that the KMT was going to take over the park tarnished that image. Since 2008, the KMT's Council of Cultural Affairs has begun a campaign to erase this memorial and other unpleasant reminders of their unsavory past. Instead of a museum honoring the victims of the White Terror, the old detention center is now an art center.

Hardly more than a month after returning from Taiwan, I learned that former President Chen Shui-bian was arrested and taken from his home in handcuffs. He was subsequently found guilty of illegally sending money out of the country. The truth of the charges against Chen may never be known because his trial was fraught with irregularities as acknowledged and protested by international legal scholars. Chen's greatest sin as far as the KMT and Beijing are concerned, and for which I am convinced he received a life sentence, was his unapologetic advocacy for a free and independent Taiwan.

The conviction of Chen and what appears to be the not-so-subtle handing over of Taiwan to Beijing by the current KMT government is not the only surprise I have received since I saw Santa's smirk in the window on that December night in 2003.

With Ma as President and the KMT in full control of the government again, Dr. Peng is out of a job. At the age of eighty-eight, he is now retired with time to write his memoirs. Since my visit to Taiwan in 2003, Peter and I have stayed in regular contact. He has been kind enough to read and comment on this manuscript.

When drafting the account of the Abe affair that resulted in our arrest, Peter and I discussed at length whether it had been a setup by the KMT or a plan by supporters of Taiwanese independence outside to send Hsieh potassium chlorate that was discovered by authorities. I discounted the latter possibility because I couldn't believe that supporters of Taiwan independence would send me the material without mine or Hsieh's consent.

One person who might have known was Yén Gench'ang, head of the printers' union and with whom Abe left the "gift" for us, but Yén had died three years before. As we talked, Peter suggested that one man might know: Munakata Takayuki. He was on the Japanese WUFI (World United Formosans for Independence) staff and worked with us to get Peter out of the country. Since I speak no Japanese and Munakata speaks no English, I had not considered asking him, even when I met him in Taiwan in 2003 and in 2008. Peter agreed that if the WUFI was involved in such a plan, Munakata would likely know. I made up a list of questions that Peter translated into Japanese and faxed to Munakata.

Peter didn't hear from Munakata until June 4. He translated Munakata's letter and sent it to me. The words were on the screen in front of me, but my mind refused to process what Peter had written. Munakata wrote that he and Peter had hatched the plan. Munakata quoted a letter from Peter dated December 10, 1970, saying, "Please just say give the chemical to Tony through Japanese friend, the details I have already told you." Concerned about moles in the WUFI, the project was known only to Peng and Munakata.

Munakata confirmed details of sending the potassium chlorate by a courier named Abe. Abe arrived in Taiwan February 16, 1971, and met with Mr. Yén at his home. According to Munakata, Abe had no idea what was in the cake, but he knew that inside was a sealed letter on very thin paper. The letter had a short paragraph in English for me that read,

> _This package is for Tony from Peter's Japanese friend; please keep it until Tony needs it._

The rest of the letter was in Japanese and addressed to Tony:

> _This is potassium chlorate, needs sulfuric acid to make explosives. Can you get sulfuric acid? If not, we can bring it in. We will tell you how to make it later. If you need anything else, tell us through Peter or contact us directly._

The letter was signed, "Munakata."

Munakata said he had no idea who "Tony" was, only that he was someone who had Peter's complete trust. Munakata told Abe that if he was in danger of being arrested, he should burn the letter or swallow it.

Abe told Mr. Yén that he had a gift for "Thornberry." Yen tried to arrange a meeting with me, but because I was unavailable he invited Judith to have lunch and pick up the gift. Mr. Yén had breakfast with Abe at his hotel on the morning of the February 18 and asked him to come for lunch with Judith. Abe was arrested at ten o'clock that morning. When he was interrogated, the officer told him that both Mr. Yén and I had been there and confessed. They gave Abe a knife and had him cut the cake. A substance that looked like sugar poured out. Abe said he didn't know what the substance was. The officer asked him if he had read the letter that was with the cake. Abe said, "The letter was sealed, so I did not read it." The officer replied, "It is explosives."

Munakata confirmed that Abe was released on Wednesday, March 3 (while we were under house arrest) and sent back to Japan. The "explosives" was a chemical easily available at any drug store in Japan, so the Japanese authorities decided that Abe had not broken any Japanese law. They took his statement and filed it.

At the end of the translation of Munakata's letter, Peter added this note:

Could you imagine my shock and surprise to discover that I myself was actually one of the culprits! I draw total blank and have not a faintest recollection of what Munakata is talking about. But since he said so, it must be so, and I owe you infinite apologies for what happened to you and Judy.

There has been voluminous correspondence between me and Munakata before and after my escape in 1970. All of them are kept in Japan and in Portland. I will search through them when I get back to Portland.

I am trying to recall what the thinking of mine and others who were involved in the independence movement was at that time. It is true at that time there was unanimous consensus that some kind of violent incidents must happen to shake up the Taiwanese people and KMT to prove that not everything is alright in Taiwan.

Though unbelievable as it may sound, it is quite possible that I was involved in some kind of violent plot. It is hard to explain the mentality or feelings of those who were fighting, at risk of their freedom or life, against the KMT of that time and their hatred of the regime.

As I said I have absolutely no recollection of this matter, but it must be the truth Munakata is telling. After I go through those correspondences of 40 years ago, I hope I can give you more details of the "plot".

Again please forgive me for all the trouble inflected on you and Judy.

After receiving Munakata's letter, Peter reviewed the correspondence and found that he had written what Munakata said.

The revelation in Munakata's letter was a complete surprise to me, and apparently no less of one to Peter. A voice within me, perhaps the voice of a child, cried out in hurt and anger because I had not been consulted about my willingness to participate in such a plan. That voice also cries out in protest because Tony, who was also not consulted, suffered in ways that scarred his body and spirit for the rest of his life.

Overshadowing the question of why I was not asked about my willingness to participate was a larger one. What would I have said had I been asked? Would I have been willing to pass on materials that someone else could use to make explosives? I had always been clear that I would not be party to violence that would cause innocent people to suffer. But if Peter, the person I trusted more than any other about the reality in Taiwan, had asked me, it would be disingenuous for me to say that I know I would have refused. After all these years, there is no way to know what I would have said.

But there was never a question about forgiving my old friend. Peter didn't have to contact Munakata for me, and he certainly could have edited Munakata's response knowing I would never know the difference. But Peter contacted him as I requested; he faithfully translated Munakata's answers to my questions; he verified them by searching through his own letters; and after we learned what happened, he insisted that I write the truth. In advancing age, I find others' memory lapses more understandable and certainly forgivable. Peter's acknowledgement of responsibility upon hearing from Munakata, whose account he trusted even before he verified the account in his own correspondence, was evidence of the great man he is.

On March 27, 1964, I was in Boston preparing to go to Taiwan. I had read the story of the murder of Catherine "Kitty" Genovese two weeks earlier outside her home in Queens, New York.[26] The reason a murder in New York was

---

[26] *New York Times*, March 27, 1964. See also A. M. Rosenthall, *Thirty-Eight Witnesses: The Kitty Genovese Case* (1964),

news in Boston was that she had been stabbed repeatedly for thirty minutes while she screamed for help. She had been heard by many of her neighbors, but only after the killer had left in his car and returned ten minutes later to finish the job did one person call the police. It became a national story of shame for those who heard and done nothing. The "bystander effect" or the "Genovese syndrome" became the name for the social psychological phenomenon in which individuals do not offer help in an emergency situation when other people are present.

New to the urban northeast, it was easy for me to blame the neighbors in Queens; but my own conscience warned, *they* could be *me*. I was haunted by the picture of Kitty Genovese's face. Indeed, I wondered if I was the "they" by leaving the United States in the midst of the struggle for civil rights and the beginning of the antiwar movement. My course had been set and I didn't change it, but I carried Kitty Genovese's image with me. In the reality I encountered in Taiwan, I couldn't understand how so many missionaries, American students, U.S. military, and embassy personnel who heard the cries of the Taiwanese people could rationalize their inaction in ways not so dissimilar from the neighbors of Kitty Genovese.

When President Nixon and Henry Kissinger met with Chou En-lai in 1973, it wasn't as if they didn't know about the human rights abuses or the corruption of the government in Taiwan. Kissinger and Peng had been in seminars together at Harvard. The president and secretary of state's justification for disregarding the legitimate interests of the Taiwanese people was what they considered the "greater good" for the interests of the United States by establishing diplomatic relations with the People's Republic of China. I had long supported establishing relations with China, but never at the expense of the Taiwanese people.

The Shanghai Communiqué was a case study in Reinhold Niebuhr's principle stating that institutions by their nature do not have the capacity to act morally—to do the right thing when it conflicts with self-interest.[27] In the

Berkley: University of California Press, 1999.
[27] *Moral Man Immoral Society*

United States and its allies' desire to accommodate the People's Republic, the de facto independence of Taiwan is once again threatened by self-interest masked as the "greater good."

Individuals, argued Niebuhr, have the capability to act morally—to do the right thing even if it conflicts with their own self-interest. I might have relegated that principle to the bone pile of idealistic but unrealistic theories had I not seen it lived out by my closest Taiwanese friends—Peng Ming-min, Wei T'ing-chao, and Hsieh Tsung-min. Although not ostensibly religious, their actions demonstrated the ideals of justice and mercy I associated with Christian life. They were living examples of the core Christian teaching I learned as a child as expressed in Jesus' parable of the Good Samaritan (or the Good Neighbor).[28] What I had seen in the failure to act by the neighbors of Kitty Genovese was the antithesis of that teaching.

"You are a guest in another country," was the oft-quoted dictum to justify not getting involved in the political affairs of a country not your own. The principle has some merit in international relations, but it is a principle that serves the status quo. As desirable as that may be in the world of nations, the principle may also be an immoral rationalization. In Taiwan, a brutal and corrupt government was enabled to stay in power due in no small measure to the support it received from the United States. I love my country and I loved the work the church had sent me to Taiwan to do, but my conscience didn't allow the luxury of being politically uninvolved. By doing nothing, I believed I was putting my stamp of approval on what the U.S. government was doing there. As an act of faith, I chose otherwise.

---

[28] Christian Bible, *Luke 10:25-37.*

Acknowledgments

If you've read this far you know that this is a book I never thought I would write. For over thirty years I didn't dare because I didn't want to endanger the Taiwanese with whom I collaborated and who were still in Taiwan. Over the years, my kids – Liz, Richard, and Katy – pestered me to write the story down, if not for publication, for them. Katy, the youngest and the only one not born in Taiwan, was the more persistent. At a sports bar in Atlanta in 2001, she made her strongest pitch, and for the first time I agreed to write something for their eyes only. Sixteen letters later, I had written an account that became the first draft for this work. Their mother, Judith Thomas, from whom I have been divorced for over twenty five years, graciously read the chapters as they were being written and commented. She remembered some things that I didn't.

Even after my first trip back to Taiwan in 2003 as a guest of the Taiwan Foundation for Democracy when the role Judith and I played in Dr. Peng's escape was first made public, I wasn't sure that I would write a book. Only in 2008, during a second trip to speak at a human rights conference commemorating Peng Ming-min, Hsieh Tsung-min, and Wei Ting-chao's 1964 publication of the "Manifesto" that landed them in prison, did I decide that the time had come.

Historian and journalist, James Wang, was also one of the presenters at the conference. He encouraged me to write the story and offered to help gather material from the National Archives in Washington D.C near where he lives. His efforts provided me with a treasure trove of declassified State Department documents. In Taiwan, journalist Sean Lu sifted through newspaper accounts of bombings in Taiwan in 1970 and 1971.

Dr. Peng encouraged me from the start as did Hsieh. They both read the manuscript and made suggestions throughout. Hsieh provided numerous documents, both about his imprisonment and torture, as well as material on current realities in Taiwan. Chang Hsin-yi interviewed Wei's wife, Chiang Ching-hui, for me. She provided important information about Wei's life after 1971.

These friends graciously read the manuscript, corrected spelling and grammatical errors, and made suggestions for content revision: Chuck and Jan Halligan, Frank and Lorraine Zachary, Jim Campbell, Ken Krieg, Phyllis Stuewig, and Richard Kagan. More than proof readers, they were cheer leaders for the project.

From start to finish my greatest cheer leader was my wife Connie. Approaching precarious surgery and in considerable discomfort as I completed the umpteenth draft of the whole book last spring, she insisted on completing her job as the last editor until a publisher took over. She could, and did, tell me things my friends were more reluctant to point out; but most of all, she believed in me and was determined that when we turned it over to a publisher it would be the best we could make it.

Convinced that the story was worth telling and getting out quickly, Lawrence Knorr of Sunbury Press, Inc. became my publisher. Artist Alecia Nye took a rough idea for a cover and created something that made me run around the house exclaiming, "That's it! That's it!" Editor Susan Hills has done what all good editors do; make the author say, "That's exactly what I meant. Why didn't I say it that way in the first place?" And she did it in record time. Marketing and Publicity's Christina Steffy and David Reimer have had the task of getting this book before the right audiences. The Sunbury staff probably does this for every book project, but they've made me feel that getting this book out was their top priority.

For all those whose labors have made this work possible, I am deeply grateful.

- Milo Thornberry
February 3, 2011
Bend, Oregon

Bibliography

American Rhetoric: Top 100 Speeches. Kennedy, John F. "Address to the Greater Houston Ministerial Association" delivered 12 September 1960 at the Rice Hotel in Houston, TX. Accessed February 15, 2009. http://www.americanrhetoric.com/speeches/jfkhoustonministers.html

Anderson, Courtney. *To the Golden Shore: the Life of Adoniram Judson.* Boston: Little, Brown, and Company, 1956.

Arrigo, Linda Gail and Lynn Miles. *A Borrowed Voice: Taiwan Human Rights Through International Networks, 1960-1980.* Taipei: Hanyao Color Printing Co, 2008.

Axelbank, Albert. "Chiang Kai-Shek's Silent Enemies." *Harper's Magazine,* September 1963.

Barnett, A. Doak. *Our China Policy: The Need for Change.* Headline Series, No. 204. Foreign Policy Association, 1971.

Brandon, S. G. F. *Jesus and the Zealots: A Study of the Political Factor in Primitive Christianity.* Manchester: Manchester University Press, 1967.

Chen, Lung-chu Chen, and Harold D. Lasswell. *Formosa, China, and the United Nations: Formosa in the World Community.* New York: St. Martin's Press, 1967.

Durdin, Peggy. "Terror in Taiwan." *The Nation.* March 24, 1947

Durdin, Tillman. "Formosa Killings Are Put at 10,000." *New York Times,* March 29, 1947.

Friedman, Edward. "Peking and Washington: Is Taiwan the Obstacle?" In *China and Ourselves,* edited by B. Douglass and Ross Terril. Boston: Beacon Press, 1970.

Harrison, Selig. "Taiwan Becoming Dilemma for U.S." *Washington Post,* March 7, 1971.

Hsieh, Tsung-min. "From a Taiwan Prison." *New York Times,* April 24, 1972.

Kagan, Richard. "Why Taiwan?" Paper presented at the Taiwan Foundation for Democracy's Conference on Democracy and Human Rights, Taipei, Taiwan, December 8-9, 2003.

Kahn, E.J., Jr. *The China Hands: America's Foreign Service Officers and What Befell Them.* New York: Viking Press, 1975.

Karsen, Wendell. "Taiwan: The Struggle for Human Rights - Memoirs of a Foreign Participant, 1969-1984." Paper presented at the Taiwan Foundation for Democracy's Conference on Democracy and Human Rights, Taipei, Taiwan, December 8-9, 2003.

Kerr, George H. *Formosa Betrayed.* New York: Houghton-Mifflin Company, 1965.

Li, Laura Tyson. *Madame Chiang Kai-shek: China's Eternal First Lady.* Boston: Atlantic Monthly Press, 2006.

Li, Thian-hok. "The China Impasse: A Formosan View." *Foreign Affairs Quarterly,* April 1958.

Mancall, Mark, ed. *Formosa Today.* New York: Praeger, 1964.

Morris, Colin. *Unyoung Uncolored Unpoor.* Nashville: Abingdon Press, 1969.

Munro, Eleanor C. *Through the Vermilion Gates: A Journey Into China's Past.* New York: Pantheon Books, 1971.

Niebuhr, Reinhold. *Moral Man and Immoral Society: A Study in Ethics and Politics.* New York: Charles Scribner's Sons, 1932.

Peng, Ming-min. *Taste of Freedom: Memoirs of a Formosan Independence Leader.* New York: Holt, Rinehart and Winston, 1972.

Rosenthall, A. M. *Thirty-Eight Witnesses: The Kitty Genovese Case.* Berkley: University of California Press, 1999.

Spartacus Educational. John Simkin on the Sit In Movement. Accessed February 16, 2009. *http://www.spartacus.schoolnet.co.uk/USAsitin.htm*

Taidoku. Jean Lin's Psycho-Political Portrait of Hsieh Tsung-Min. Accessed June 20, 2009. *http://taidoku.fc2web.com/ouen102.htm#introduction*

Taiwan Foundation for Democracy. *A Journey of Remembrance and Appreciation: International Friends and Taiwan's Democracy and Human Rights.* Papers presented at the Taiwan Foundation for Democracy's Conference on Democracy and Human Rights, Taipei, Taiwan, December 8-9, 2003.

Thelin, Virginia and Mark. "Our Contributions Toward Democracy in Taiwan." Paper presented at the Taiwan Foundation for Democracy's Conference on Democracy and Human Rights, Taipei, Taiwan, December 8-9, 2003.

Thomas, Judith and Milo Thornberry. "Helping Peng Ming-min Escape: We Must Oppose the Oppression Our Country Is Supporting, Else We are Complicit." In *A Borrowed Voice: Taiwan Human Rights Through International Networks, 1960-1980,* written/edited by Lindai Gail Arrigo and Lynn Miles, 179-186. Taipei: Hanyao Color Printing Co, 2008.

Thornberry, Judith and Milo. *China, Taiwan and Christian Responsibility.* New York: Joint Commission on Education and Cultivation of the Board of Missions of The United Methodist Church, 1971.

Thornberry, Judith and Milo. "Taiwan: Third Factor in the China Problem." *Christianity and Crisis*, June 28, 971.

Thornberry, Milo and Judith Thomas. "Our Human Rights Activities in Taiwan." Paper presented at the Taiwan Foundation for Democracy's Conference on Democracy and Human Rights, Taipei, Taiwan, December 8-9, 2003.

Thornberry, Milo L. "American Missionaries and the Chinese Communists: A Study of Views Expressed by Methodist Episcopal Church Missionaries, 1921-1941." Th.D. diss., Boston University, 1974.

Van Es, Judy and Rowland. "Repressed Memories: Soldiers Standing Every 10-20 Yards on the Route to the Airport." In *A Borrowed Voice: Taiwan Human Rights Through International Networks, 1960-1980,* written/edited by Lindai Gail Arrigo and Lynn Miles, 197-201. Taipei: Hanyao Color Printing Co, 2008) p. 197.

Van Es, Judy and Rowland. "Rowland and Judy Van Es." Paper presented at the Taiwan Foundation for Democracy's Conference on Democracy and Human Rights, Taipei, Taiwan, December 8-9, 2003.

Wedemeyer, Albert Coady. "The Nationalist Occupation of Formosa," In *Foreign Relations of the United States 1947. The Far East: China.* Volume VII. Washington D.C.: U.S. Government Printing Office, 1947.

White, Theodore H., and Annalee Jacoby. *Thunder Out of China.* New York: William Sloane Associates, Inc. 1946.

Wilson, Donald J. "Donald J. Wilson, 1959-1967." Paper presented at the Taiwan Foundation for Democracy's Conference on Democracy and Human Rights, Taipei, Taiwan, December 8-9, 2003.

Made in the USA
Lexington, KY
04 April 2011